T0073086

Beginner's Guide to Code Algorithms

Beginner's Guide to Code Algorithms

Experiments to Enhance Productivity and Solve Problems

by Deepankar Maitra

CRC Press
Taylor & Francis Group
Boca Raton London New York

CRC Press is an imprint of the
Taylor & Francis Group, an informa business

First edition published 2022
by CRC Press
6000 Broken Sound Parkway NW, Suite 300, Boca Raton, FL 33487-2742

and by CRC Press
2 Park Square, Milton Park, Abingdon, Oxon, OX14 4RN

CRC Press is an imprint of Taylor & Francis Group, LLC

Library of Congress Cataloging-in-Publication Data
Names: Maitra, Deepankar, author.
Title: Beginner's guide to code algorithms : experiments to enhance
productivity and solve problems / Deepankar Maitra.
Description: First edition. | Boca Raton : CRC Press, [2022] |
Includes bibliographical references and index. |
Summary: "This book takes you on a problem-solving journey to expand your mind and
increase your willingness to experiment with code"– Provided by publisher.
Identifiers: LCCN 2021044911 (print) | LCCN 2021044912 (ebook) |
ISBN 9781032080642 (hbk) | ISBN 9781032102382 (pbk) | ISBN 9781003214335 (ebk)
Subjects: LCSH: Computer algorithms–Amateurs' manuals. |
Application software–Development–Amateurs' manuals. |
Computer programming–Amateurs' manuals.
Classification: LCC QA76.9.A43 M34 2022 (print) |
LCC QA76.9.A43 (ebook) | DDC 005.1–dc23
LC record available at https://lccn.loc.gov/2021044911
LC ebook record available at https://lccn.loc.gov/2021044912

ISBN: 978-1-032-08064-2 (hbk)
ISBN: 978-1-032-10238-2 (pbk)
ISBN: 978-1-003-21433-5 (ebk)

DOI: 10.1201/9781003214335

Typeset in Times
by Newgen Publishing UK

Additional eResources for this book are available for download at:
https://www.routledge.com/Beginners-Guide-to-Code-Algorithms-Experiments-to-Enhance-
Productivity/Maitra/p/book/9781032102382

For my parents
Mr. Priyanath and Mrs. Geeta Maitra
Dr. Amiya Prosad and Mrs. Durga Majumdar

Contents

Contents

Preface

People talk about AI, VR, AR, etc. these days. Each term has a deep scientific meaning and sociopolitical connotation for the user of these words and the people they are directed to. It is simply amazing to see how loosely these terms are used and interpreted today. For example, the A in the AI stands for artificial. While people generally understand that AI is artificial intelligence, I have come across a variety of ways that people perceive "artificial". Is it the capability of a machine to figure a problem? Or is it an ability for a device to do a task? The fact is neither—AI is a computer science term intended to mean the ability of machines to develop "intelligence" much the same way as humans—the capability to "learn".

In this book, I want to introduce a new concept—augmented common sense (ACS). This is in effect the opposite of AI in some sense—it is the ability of humans to develop common sense with the help of machines! Simple concept. Powerful implications for your specific universe—I deliberately chose the word "universe" because I did not want to limit the vast number of situations the average human goes through. Work. Leisure. Entertainment. Exercise. Nurture. Innovate. Contribute. These are all situations that require humans to apply their common sense.

The materials presented here will help you to strengthen your logic and develop your ability to write simple programs to automate your tasks. While there are innumerable ways that a human endeavor can be improved, I will be discussing how this can be achieved through the use of spreadsheets. You will need:

- A computer
- Microsoft Office (any version)
- Your basic skill in working with a spreadsheet
- Your desire to learn programming

The last one is scary for some and easy for others. This book is intended for those who want to be inspired to develop their ACS through programming and discover the beauty of logic—the happiness of solving a riddle.

After reading this book, I hope to have elevated your appreciation of programming. But that is just a side effect. My main objective is to entertain. To help you see the beauty of common sense and to appreciate how simple computing can make mundane tasks interesting.

I am going to begin with a discussion on algorithms and quickly transition into some real-life examples that are both entertaining and useful. Starting with a program on how to play Tic Tac Toe with the computer, I am going to describe a few other interesting problems hoping to inspire you to try your own. The last chapter is a more complex discussion on writing a program to draw a COVID graph of USA—developed from the common question that we found ourselves hurled into in 2020, during the tough pandemic days.

Albert Einstein had two famous quotes.

Two things are infinite: the universe and human stupidity; and I'm not sure about the universe.

– Albert Einstein

I am enough of an artist to draw freely upon my imagination. Imagination is more important than knowledge. Knowledge is limited. Imagination encircles the world.

– Albert Einstein

This book is to help you discover the world of smart applications through the power of your limitless imagination.

Let the fun begin!

Acknowledgments

I am grateful to Dr. Anil Bhowmick for his continued encouragement and support.

I thank Dr. Ananda Datta, Venki Krishnamoorthy, and Satish Badgi for their constructive comments and suggestions.

I want to recognize my daughters—Aparajita for the illustration in Chapter 10 and Amrapali for reviewing the initial chapters.

I appreciate my son-in-law Lahiru for the infinite snacks and granddaughter Anika for her inspiring smiles.

For editing my manuscript and keeping my dream alive—I thank my wife Saswati.

Author Biography

Deepankar Maitra is a leader in business software solution architecture, focused on Human Capital Management. For the past 30 years, he has managed the implementation of enterprise applications in multinational corporations, providing digital solutions to a userbase of over 2,000,000.

A valedictorian and a National Talent Scholar, Deepankar is devoted to helping the new generation of consultants demystify technology and simplify complex business scenarios. His philosophy of creating impact through knowledge-sharing has evolved into teaching courses, presenting at international conferences, and developing guides for technology professionals.

Deepankar's consulting journey started in New Zealand, where he worked with leading business software vendors to enhance their products. His algorithmic solutions were implemented by several industries such as airlines, improving low lead time aircraft maintenance, repair, and overhaul processes.

A graduate of the premier Indian Institute of Technology, Deepankar has a passion for solving the world's most complex riddles and believes in practicing brainteasers for mental fitness. Through this book, he wants to inspire readers to tap into a world of possibilities using code.

Deepankar currently lives in Houston, TX and works as an executive in a leading international consulting firm.

Introduction

The earth rotates around its axis every 23 hours, 56 minutes, and 4 seconds. We call this a day and then, before we know it, the calendar automatically changes its date to the next day. A day is never enough to get everything done! If we pause for a moment and think about the tasks we could not complete, quite often it is because they are repetitive and high in volume. Repetitive tasks throw a damper to our spirits—especially if they are numerous. A task that needs to be done again and again is no longer interesting, and mentally we are ready to move on to something different, even if it is simply to relieve the drudgery.

Take for example an analyst who needs to compile a financial report with 600 lines of amounts in a single currency. Yes, the currency conversion table is available in a spreadsheet, but the rate changes every day. The analyst needs to do this boring task of downloading the rate from a website and fitting it into a table, adjusting "vlookups" and confirming that the amounts are all converted correctly—manual tasks have chances of error and the only way to assure their accuracy is through spending even more time checking them.

Take another example where a survey is launched and the budget inputs for different departments all come in separate forms—there is no quick way to merge them into one spreadsheet although the formats are the same.

We have a robot. We can use the robot to do a great deal of the repetitive work. If only we knew how to train it!

Yes, I am talking about the laptop we own. It has come a long way from the first computer ENIAC. Invented in 1943, it had 18,000 vacuum tubes and occupied 1,800 square feet of space. The modern-day laptop takes the speed of ENIAC from about 400 instructions per second to several billion—that is quite impressive in terms of speed. But what good is the speed if we cannot use it to solve our daily problems and reduce the time we spend on our boring tasks? We have our speedy computer but how do we harness its power? How do we explain to our speedy computer—the untrained robot—the problems we want help with?

This is the theme of the book. How to train your robot by a combination of common sense, algorithmic skills, and a bit of coding. And have some fun along the way! You will find immense joy in creating your ideas and helping others with the code you develop!

This book is not about teaching you the syntax of coding—for that, there are manuals available online that you can refer to. (I have provided some links at the end of this book.) Unlike a traditional computer programming book, I have covered the essential programming techniques in simple and fun ways for you to experiment and learn. The techniques are by no means exhaustive, but sufficient for you to get inspired, learn coding, and enjoy the process! They are explained in an increasing order of complexity to help you develop your skill of coding an algorithm in progressive steps.

DOI: 10.1201/9781003214335-1

Throughout the book, the emphasis is for you to find a practical solution by using simple concepts and reusing code that you will find in this book. You will find here working code for several interesting scenarios and you can use these as building blocks for your own personalized solutions.

Chapter 1 introduces the concept of algorithms and presents this learning as the heart of all computing endeavors. It discusses the origins of the word and explains it in simple terms.

Chapter 2 takes you through a step-by-step process to create a game that almost everyone has played in their childhood—thus establishing the main principles of writing a program with a simple introduction to user interfaces. This is the second longest chapter that lays the foundation for teaching a few more advanced skills that are presented in the following chapters. The biggest barrier to program development is the fear of failure—this fear paralyzes most individuals who are not in the computing profession. The techniques described in this chapter will help get over this fear by teaching you how to "debug" your program—no matter how small—and understand which part is not working, so that it can be quickly corrected and lead you to a successful run.

Chapter 3 describes how to automate a very popular puzzle—Sudoku. This chapter teaches a few new skills such as discovering patterns based on tuples and exploring deductive logic to solve a complex riddle. Sudoku is fun. But solving Sudoku by developing algorithms for each technique is ten times more fun!

Chapter 4 discusses the concept of multiplatform integration by introducing a problem of controlling a powerpoint presentation from a smartphone and then solving it through simple programming techniques. It also demonstrates that innovation can be achieved in simple things if you put your mind to it.

Chapter 5 teaches how to handle files through a very innovative exercise—creating a filing cabinet for your computer files while introducing the concept of recursion.

Chapter 6 discusses the workbook merge problem—how to combine multiple sheets into one without having to open each one and manually cut and paste. While the code is simple, it saves a lot of time and repetitive effort.

Chapter 7 introduces the topic of graphs by teaching you how to convert three columns of text to a graphical architecture diagram automatically, through the use of the spreadsheet. This program is a very useful tool for system engineers to visualize how data are exchanged between different components of a complex system.

Chapter 8 builds on the graphical concepts of Chapter 6 by solving the reverse problem—how to convert a graph to text.

Chapter 9 teaches a fundamental technique of web scraping—a skill that is essential for automating all kinds of tasks that need pulling data from the web. It teaches the complex part of pulling these data where data retrieval requires a "prompt" (e.g., a form) and reveals how to automate this prompt.

Chapter 10 explores the character of Professor Butts and Rube Goldberg machines. Through a simple example of a webcam software, it helps you build a burglar alarm, a customer counter, a remotely activated camera, and a greeting machine. These examples should serve as an inspiration for you to experiment with simple programming concepts that you can connect and build, unraveling a legoland of opportunities.

Chapter 11 pulls in all the skills learnt in the previous chapters to create a visualization that is complex, relevant, and complete.

The book is not meant to be a formal theoretical dissertation. Each chapter is an experiment—a story of success where a human being was able to build something awesome by using the power of Excel on your laptop and a little bit of coding. The original codes in this book are written by me on a Windows computer, but they would work on Macs as well with very few, if any, compatibility issues.

The code provided in this book is written in a simple way that does not confuse the reader with complex computer science rigors of efficient coding. There are no materials that are devoted to explain good coding practices, best ways to name variables, quickest way to do a sort or the explanation of memory management. These are important—but the emphasis here is on how to solve a problem with a quick and intuitive way to code the algorithm. There are many books available for the "science", but very few on the "art" of solving.

You may ultimately want to be a developer and even a computer scientist but right now all you need is to understand the technique of building an algorithm.

The code used in this book is available for you to download on the publisher's site, along with a few videos on some chapters to get you started.

To maximize your learning, you have to practice the code, test it out yourself, and build it further to address your specific needs.

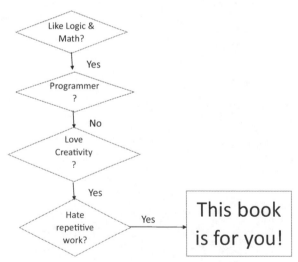

FIGURE I.1   Algorithm of this book.

1 What Is an Algorithm?

Algorithm is a word used in computer science. It simply means a step-by-step instruction. But it encapsulates the essence of computer programming, because without a step-by-step instruction a computer cannot perform a useful task. Therefore, it means much more than that.

The word algorithm has the same root as the word Algebra. With an Arab past, it came from ninth-century Persian mathematician Muḥammad ibn Mūsā al-Khwārizmī. Al-Khwārizmī (Arabic: الخوارزمی, c. 780–850) was a Persian mathematician, astronomer, geographer, and scholar whose name means "the native of Khwarazm", a region that was part of Greater Iran and is now in Uzbekistan.

About 825 AD, al-Khwarizmi wrote an Arabic language treatise on the Hindu–Arabic numeral system, which was translated into Latin during the 12th century under the title Algoritmi de numero Indorum. This title means "Algoritmi on the numbers of the Indians", where "Algoritmi" was the translator's Latinization of al-Khwarizmi's name. The modern sense of this word was introduced in the 19th century. By the way, al-Khwarizmi was the most widely read mathematician in Europe in the late Middle Ages, primarily through another of his books, the Algebra.

Algorithms are part of our understanding of life and is used by all fields and disciplines to convey a process. Some are small and famous. Like the book "Eat, Love, Pray". Or the recent hotel/restaurant ad: "Eat, Drink, Sleep, Repeat". Some are long and detailed, such as a recipe.

In the computer world, an algorithm is used to code the program, hence needs to be somewhat detailed. But the role of the algorithm is to facilitate the creation of the program—just like a recipe. Once the chocolate chip cookie is made, the recipe is not useful, until you are ready to make the next batch!

The discussion on algorithms is not complete without the concept of some important attributes . A good algorithm needs to be:

- Accurate
- Repeatable
- Concise
- Optimized

DOI: 10.1201/9781003214335-2

How to make chocolate chip cookies

Ingredients
- 2 cups all-purpose flour
- 1 teaspoon baking soda
- Fine salt
- 1 stick (12 tablespoons) unsalted butter, at room temperature
- 1 cup packed light brown sugar
- 1 cup granulated sugar
- 2 large eggs
- 1 teaspoon pure vanilla extract
- One 12-ounce bag semisweet chocolate chips

Process
1. Preheat to 375 degrees F
2. Stir together the flour, baking soda, and 1 teaspoon salt in a large bowl.
3. Beat the butter and both sugars, eggs, vanilla, and flour about 4 minutes. Stir in the chocolate chips.
4. Scoop 12 tablespoons of dough about 2 inches apart onto each prepared baking sheet. Roll the dough into balls with slightly wet hands.
5. Bake, rotating the cookie sheets from upper to lower racks halfway through, until golden but still soft in the center, 12 to 15 minutes.
6. Wait for a few minutes on the baking sheet, and then transfer to a rack to cool completely.

FIGURE 1.1   Making chocolate chip cookies.

These four qualities can be easily understood with the recipe example.

The recipe is accurate, in the sense that it can create **tasty** chocolate chip cookies. Note the emphasis on "tasty". The recipe does not create "healthy" cookies. For that matter, the word "healthy" has its own set of attributes, which are somewhat subjective (does healthy mean less carb? More protein? Less cholesterol? More vitamins?) and mutually interdependent (higher magnesium and phosphorus in a readily available ingredient like brown sugar may also mean higher carb).

Repeatable is easily demonstrated by being able to use the recipe again and again for making delicious cookies. A recipe would not be so repeatable if it requires an ingredient that is tough to procure. Or sometimes the product is self-destructive, which does not make it repeatable. A good example of a self-destructive algorithm is a video shoot of an accident.

Concise is a quality of being able to express in a few words. For example, I want to say that I suffer from a problem where my lens in my right eye is unable to focus light beyond a distance in front of my retina. I can express it with the term "myopia". While this is just a better way to communicate in this instance, for an algorithm that is concise, it can have a huge consequence, such as reduce the cost of producing a vaccine by 50% or increase the chances striking oil in the ground by 30%.

The dictionary meaning of "optimized" is "make the best or most effective use of a situation, opportunity, or resource". Optimized is a quality that is the hardest to understand. Optimized can mean many things based on the "situation, opportunity or resource" that is optimized. For example, the Tesla model 3 is the most fuel-efficient car in the "midsize" class of cars in 2020, as determined by fueleconomy.gov. Note that I had to qualify this statement by the year and the "class". Even in 2020, the most fuel-efficient class of "compact" cars is not Tesla—it is Volkswagen e-Golf. And the most fuel-efficient "midsize" car in 2015 was Nissan Leaf.

The point I want you to take away from this discussion is that no good quality is an absolute value. True for life as well, the qualities that make the evaluation of anything "good" or "bad" are bound by the parameters that are used to judge them.

We will discuss these qualities further in the next few chapters, as we dive deep into the programs that I will introduce to get you inspired.

So why do we need algorithms?

Algorithms are to program development what a recipe is to the preparation of a dish—a bit more in some respects and a bit less in others.

An algorithm for a program describes how the code needs to be written in conceptual terms.

Even though there is no precise measurement like a recipe, an algorithm is a documentation of technique that is indispensable for the programmer. Just as you cannot make cookies without a recipe, you cannot write a program that solves a specific problem without an algorithm.

An algorithm usually has six parts to it:

- Inputs
- Outputs
- Variables
- Statements
- Conditional Statements
- Repetitions

The input is what is available for the processor to work with—for example, the flour and the sugar.

The output is the cookie but can be other things as well, such as a timer that chimes when the cooking is done (audible output), or the mixers and plates that need to be washed after the cookie is made (visible outputs).

Variables are receptacles that temporarily store something so that you can remember it or use it later on. For example, you have a glass of water and you need to use only half of it now and half later. You will need another glass to pour the other half until you need it. Now suppose that you do not have a measuring stick to measure the height of the glass, and you do not want to rely on your judgment to determine whether it is exactly half—what do you do? You get another glass that looks exactly like the other two glasses. You pour the full glass into the two empty ones and check their heights by placing them side by side. If one is higher, you pour a little bit from the glass with the greater height to the glass with the lesser height.

A statement is usually an instruction to do something—the most common being moving data from one variable to another. In the glass example above, pouring water from one glass to another in an attempt to equalize is a statement.

A condition is a decision point that helps the situation direct the execution of a statement from a choice of more than one statement. In our example above, checking the water level in one glass is higher than the other is a condition. That helps one decide whether to pour the water from the left glass to the right, or from the right glass to the left. Pouring water from one glass to another is a conditional statement. Pouring from left to right is one statement, from right to left is another, and the condition helps us decide which one should be done.

Chances are that just one pour will not equalize the glasses. If you are like me, as soon as I have poured the higher to the lower, the lower now becomes higher! So, we need to do the exact opposite, until we find that the heights are the same. This is known as a repetition. Often described in programming languages as "Do Loops", "While Loops" and "Do Untils"—this is the critical part of an algorithm that is immensely useful for a program—because it is the repetitive work that a computer program does best, by relieving the human being from this task.

Now let us look at a problem that we can solve using a spreadsheet to understand these six structures in business terms.

Imagine that I am a sales executive in a shoe company that operates in three states. I need to send a report to my boss that summarizes the sales for all three states in one spreadsheet. I have each state in a separate spreadsheet as shown below.

	A	B	C
1	From 1-Jan21 to 31-Jan-21		
2	STATE	SHOE TYPE	QUANTITY
3	Texas	Trendy Trainer	100
4	Texas	Jazzy Jogger	250
5	Texas	Rustic Runner	300
6	Texas	Wobbly Walker	23
7	Texas	Shaggy Stroller	5
8			

SPREADSHEET A

FIGURE 1.2   Sales figures by state.

	A	B	C
1	From 1-Jan21 to 31-Jan-21		
2	STATE	SHOE TYPE	QUANTITY
3	Massachusetts	Trendy Trainer	50
4	Massachusetts	Jazzy Jogger	23
5	Massachusetts	Rustic Runner	523
6	Massachusetts	Wobbly Walker	34
7	Massachusetts	Shaggy Stroller	45
8			

SPREADSHEET B

	A	B	C
1	From 1-Jan21 to 31-Jan-21		
2	STATE	SHOE TYPE	QUANTITY
3	New York	Trendy Trainer	34
4	New York	Jazzy Jogger	567
5	New York	Rustic Runner	23
6	New York	Wobbly Walker	123
7	New York	Shaggy Stroller	145
8			

SPREADSHEET C

FIGURE 1.2 Continued

I need to execute the following steps to make my boss happy:

1. Open a new spreadsheet
2. Copy spreadsheet A from cells A1 to C7
3. Paste this in the new spreadsheet in cell A1
4. Copy spreadsheet B from cells B1 to C7 *(note that we did not copy rows 1 and 2 again—since these are part of the header)*
5. Paste this in the new spreadsheet in cell A8 *(note that the row has now advanced to 7 in the new spreadsheet)*
6. Copy spreadsheet C from cells B1 to C7
7. Paste this in the new spreadsheet in cell A13 *(note that the row has now advanced to 12 in the new spreadsheet)*
8. Save new spreadsheet
9. Send to Boss via email

The final spreadsheet would look something like this.

	A	B	C
1	From 1-Jan21 to 31-Jan-21		
2	STATE	SHOE TYPE	QUANTITY
3	Texas	Trendy Trainer	100
4	Texas	Jazzy Jogger	250
5	Texas	Rustic Runner	300
6	Texas	Wobbly Walker	23
7	Texas	Shaggy Stroller	5
8	Massachusetts	Trendy Trainer	50
9	Massachusetts	Jazzy Jogger	23
10	Massachusetts	Rustic Runner	523
11	Massachusetts	Wobbly Walker	34
12	Massachusetts	Shaggy Stroller	45
13	New York	Trendy Trainer	34
14	New York	Jazzy Jogger	567
15	New York	Rustic Runner	23
16	New York	Wobbly Walker	123
17	New York	Shaggy Stroller	145
18			

FIGURE 1.3 Combined spreadsheet.

While this is a precise set of steps to accomplish this task, this is completely manual. If I had 50 states to deal with, this would be taking me too long! In order to teach any computer how to do this, we need to convert it to an algorithm. This is not different from the set of steps, as I mentioned before. Just a little more methodical.

Here is an algorithmic version of these steps:

1. Open a new spreadsheet
2. Repeat for each input spreadsheet
   a. Open the input spreadsheet
   b. Copy all rows used
   c. Find the first empty row in new spreadsheet
   d. Paste copied rows
3. Save new spreadsheet
4. Send to boss via email

Each of these steps can be achieved in an excel macro, including the sending of email.

What changed it from a set of steps to an algorithm? The repetition.

As I had mentioned earlier in this chapter, an algorithm has several components, but the key component is the repetition—the ability to do something again and again *in a controlled manner.*

The last four words are significant—it is as important for an algorithm to know how to repeat, as it is to understand when to stop. In the previous example, if it keeps pasting the copied rows without stopping that would make the new spreadsheet unnaturally big and the boss very unhappy. The problem of combining spreadsheets into one is discussed in more detail with instructions on how to convert this algorithm to real code in Chapter 6.

The next few chapters will develop this concept of algorithms with more complex and interesting problems. The art of developing an algorithm cannot be taught. It is a little bit like swimming—it is a skill that can only be learned by plunging yourself in the water. The examples you will find in this book will hopefully serve you well as a life jacket as they take you through a variety of situations from everyday life.

2 Build Your Own Game with a Simple Algorithm
Tic Tac Toe

Let me begin.

You have a computer and a spreadsheet application (Excel).

You are already good at Excel—so what is there new to learn here?

There is a gold mine of opportunity hidden away in your laptop.

Starting to write a program when you have never written one should not be scary. But strangely enough, this thought is scary for many people I have met. This is explainable and psychologists say that the reasons are one of the following:

- Fear of doing something new
- Fear of breaking something
- Fear of failure

So let me begin by dispelling all of them at once by a simple experiment.

2.1 HOW TO GET STARTED

Start your computer. Open up the Excel application. Open a new sheet. You are on Sheet1. Enter the following:

	A	B
1	Zip Code	City
2	20001	Washington
3	22554	Stafford

FIGURE 2.1 Excel sheet.

Now click on the + sign at the bottom of your sheet near the tab name (Sheet1) and create a new sheet—this is automatically called Sheet2.

DOI: 10.1201/9781003214335-3

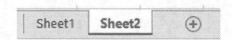

FIGURE 2.2   Sheet2.

Check your View Menu. You should see something like this:

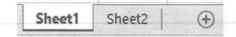

FIGURE 2.3   View Menu—Record Macro.

Click on Macros and then "Record Macro".
The system will prompt you with a name: Macro1. Just accept it and click on Ok.
The recorder is now on. Perform these three simple steps below:

1. Click on Sheet1 to come back to the original tab.

FIGURE 2.4   Sheet1.

2. Select your entered text and press Control-C.

Zip Code	City
20001	Washington
22554	Stafford

FIGURE 2.5   Control-C.

3. Switch to Sheet2. Click on the first cell (A1). Press Control-V.

	A	B
1	Zip Code	City
2	20001	Washington
3	22554	Stafford

FIGURE 2.6   Control-V.

Now stop the recorder by pressing the Stop Recorder option in the View menu.

FIGURE 2.7   Stop recording.

Voila—you now have a program that you just wrote! This language is officially called Visual Basic.

See it by going to the same View-Macro menu.

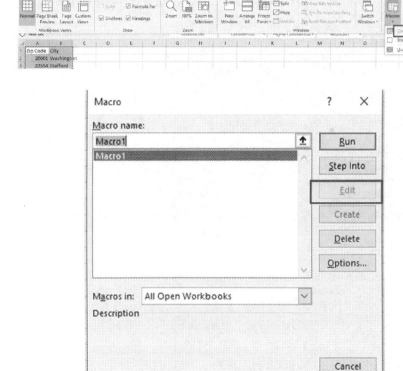

FIGURE 2.8   Macro1.

Find your macro (Macro1) and click on Edit.

You should now see your code in a different sheet (I will share a little more about this sheet in a second).

Your code should look like this:

```
Sub Macro1()
'
' Macro1 Macro
'
    Sheets("Sheet1").Select
    Range("A1:B3").Select
    Selection.Copy
    Sheets("Sheet2").Select
    ActiveSheet.Paste
End Sub
```

FIGURE 2.9   Macro1 code.

This view is the view of the Visual Basic Applications Window of excel. See the picture below. Each program is a "project" as you can have multiple programs for the same workbook. The name of the project is defined by the workbook—in this case we haven't named it yet, so it appears as Book1.

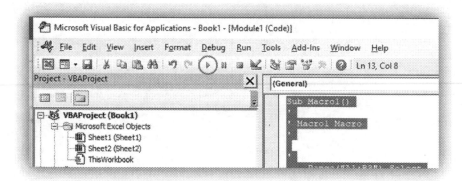

FIGURE 2.10   VBA Project.

Now you should be able to run this program.

To see it is working, erase the data we just copied into Sheet2.

Come back to the Visual Basic window and click on the play button circled in red above.

You will see that the copied text now reappears in Sheet2!

2.2   HOW TO GET WARMED UP

Let's get straight to the game now.

It is a game of Tic Tac Toe—the age-old game that has been played over the centuries. A different version of this game was played by Romans in the first century BC and it was called "Terni Lapilli" (three pebbles at a time). They played it with the same nine squares, but were restricted to using only three pieces, so had to move them around. Also found at Egyptian ruins, there is little doubt that this game has been popular in history. Tic Tac Toe has many names in other countries—it is called "Kata Kuti" in the Eastern part of India, "Exy-Ozies" in Ireland, and "Xs and Os" in Zimbabwe!

We are going to build a game of Tic Tac Toe using the Visual Basic language, using the same skills that you just demonstrated by creating Macro1!

A spreadsheet is, in my opinion, one of the world's greatest inventions. It lets you do so many things. Calculations. Formulas. Organizing data. Creating reports. Charts. The list is almost endless. It is also a great modeling tool—if you can imagine what you need in terms of business or mathematical problem, you can develop a model to build the answer. And when you apply the correct algorithm, the possibilities are endless and the outcomes surprisingly impressive, given the amount of time you need to spend. I will show you a few of these algorithms in this book. Hopefully this will motivate your imagination to model and solve your own unique business, educational, or recreational problems.

I want to show you how you can build a rudimentary game of Tic Tac Toe using what you have learnt so far.

Let us say we want to use the cells in three columns and three rows of your spread-sheet to play the game. In the figure below, this is the green-shaded area:

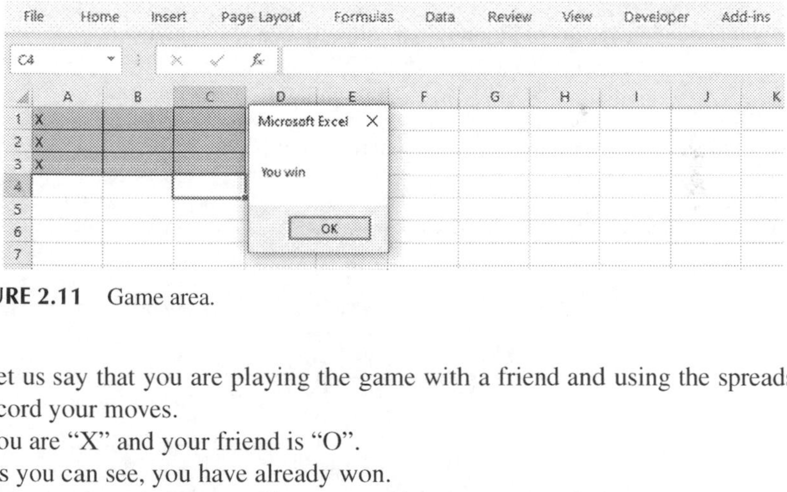

FIGURE 2.11   Game area.

Let us say that you are playing the game with a friend and using the spreadsheet to record your moves.

You are "X" and your friend is "O".

As you can see, you have already won.

This simple code below will generate this win message for you.

```
Sub Macro1()
'
' Macro1 Macro
'
If Cells(1, 1) = "X" And Cells(2, 1) = "X" And Cells(3, 1) = "X" Then
    MsgBox ("You win")
End If

End Sub
```

FIGURE 2.12   Win message code.

You can easily refer to a cell in your spreadsheet using the "Cells" function. The numbers in parenthesis refer to the row and the column. Row 1 column 1 is the cell A1 and is referred to as Cells(1,1) in the program.

Checking for a string value (alphabets or a combination of alphabets, special characters and numbers) requires the use of quotation marks. You do not need them if you are checking for numbers.

But the code is not complete. It can only detect the first column. It can only detect the "X", not the "O".

You can easily build on this code to check all columns, rows, and diagonals. If you think about it for a second, there are eight possibilities for winning for each player (three rows, three columns, and two diagonals). Hence 16 variations. You therefore need to add 15 additional statements like the one above to complete the game.

While this is fun and can be easily accomplished, there are a few drawbacks:

- It lacks visual appeal
- You have to know that the game should only be played in rows 1 to 3 and columns 1 to 3
- You need another player to play it
- Once a game is done you have to manually clean out the cells before you can play another one
- You cannot keep score
- You cannot easily extend the logic to more than a 3 × 3 matrix

This is why you need more sophisticated techniques.

Let us solve the first problem first. The visual appeal is also known as a "user interface" in computer jargon.

I am going to show you how to build something like this that looks much prettier.

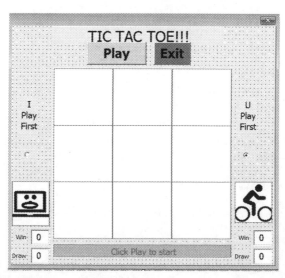

FIGURE 2.13   Tic Tac Toe user interface.

2.3   HOW TO BUILD THE SCREEN (UI, USER INTERFACE)

First, let's build a form for Tic Tac Toe.

FIGURE 2.14   Userform.

Click on "Insert" and then "UserForm".

You will see a blank screen and a toolbox

We are only going to use five controls as shown below:

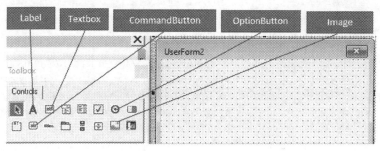

FIGURE 2.15   Form Controls.

This is going to be fun!

First, display the properties window by selecting the option under the "View" menu as shown.

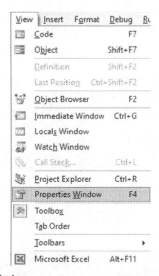

FIGURE 2.16   Properties Window.

Now use the Textbox to create the nine boxes as shown in the next picture.

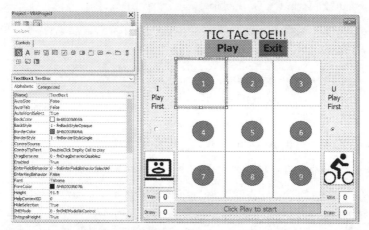

FIGURE 2.17   Creating Text Boxes in Form.

This is literally a blank canvas! I encourage you to experiment with all the different options that the toolbox and properties window present. But just for this example, I will provide the complete properties of each **TextBox**. Notice that the full list is not visible above. Hence, I will show you the rest of the properties in a separate picture in Figure 2.18.

Properties - TextBox1		×
TextBox1 TextBox		⌄

Alphabetic	Categorized	
Left	66	
Locked	False	
MaxLength	0	
MouseIcon	(None)	
MousePointer	0 - fmMousePointerDefault	
MultiLine	False	
PasswordChar		
ScrollBars	0 - fmScrollBarsNone	
SelectionMargin	True	
SpecialEffect	0 - fmSpecialEffectFlat	
TabIndex	0	
TabKeyBehavior	False	
TabStop	True	
Tag		
Text		
TextAlign	2 - fmTextAlignCenter	
Top	66	
Value		
Visible	True	
Width	96	
WordWrap	True	

FIGURE 2.18   Text Box 1.

Changing the properties of any control is easy. Simply click on the control, and the "Properties Window" on the left will show you the current set of properties and allow you to change them. You can greatly accelerate your work by using the copy (Ctrl-C) and Paste (Ctrl-V) functions. Once you have created TextBox1, simply copy and paste eight times. VBA will automatically assign the field names the numbers 2 to 9 as a suffix to keep them unique.

You do have to position them in the right place as shown in the picture, since the "Paste" function puts the text box in an odd spot on the canvas.

There are five more **TextBoxes** to add:

- TextBox10: Message bar (Default: Click Play to Start")
- TextBox11: Win score of Computer (Default 0)
- TextBox12: Win score for Human User (Default 0)
- TextBox13: Draw score for Computer (Default 0)
- TextBox14: Draw score for Human User (Default 0)

Add the default values in the "Value" property of each textbox.

Now, let's work on the remaining four controls.

The **Labels** are the easiest, since they do not have any function other than to display a name for the different parts of your canvas. There are five labels, as listed below. You should be able to create and place them in the correct positions without much difficulty. The names of the label fields are not important, since we are rarely going to refer to them in our program. But the displayed text must be entered in the "Caption" property.

- TIC TAC TOE
- I Play First
- U Play First
- Win (twice)
- Draw (twice)

The **CommandButtons** (Play and Exit) have code associated with them, which I will cover later. Just for the canvas, treat them like labels. Get the Caption filled in and color them as you please, using the "BackColor" property.

The **OptionButtons** allow you to select one of many options. There are only two in this canvas, under each label representing the two options of "I Play First" and "U Play First". There are two important properties of OptionButtons that you must know. The Value is a default that appears when you launch the form. Make sure OptionButton2 ("U Play First") has a value of true and OptionButton1 (I Play First) is False to begin the game with a default of "U Play first". The second property is the GroupName. Make sure the GroupName is set to the same value for both the OptionButtons. Yes, they can be blank.

Who is "I" or "U" in this game? Well, the idea here is that the "Computer" is presenting the game, hence Computer is "I" and the human player is "U". This is why the two images are assigned. You can attach any image you like for these two **Image** controls—they are only for show (no code association).

Now that we have built the form, let us breathe life into it.

2.4   BUILDING A "GAME" FROM A "WIDGET"

What you have so far is a widget. You enter something and the program produces something based on your input. In order to make it into a game, you need to put in a few more frills. The most important of which is a scoring system. This feeling of "win" or "loss" is what makes a widget interesting and will draw people to "play" it.

This is done by writing code. You already have a great start with Macro1. Let's go back to the code and continue to build.

Go to your Project Explorer window and double-click on Module1. If this window is not visible, simply select "Project Explorer" from the "View" menu.

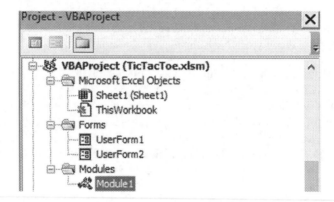

FIGURE 2.19   Project Explorer.

Let us now write the piece of code that launches the game.

This is simple—it shows the form we have created and initializes the variables we are going to use to control the game

```
Sub InitFormFirst()
   Dim cCont As Control
   UserForm1.Show
   For i = 1 To 3
     For j = 1 To 3
        UserForm1.Controls("TextBox" & (i - 1) * 3 + j) = ""
        UserForm1.Controls("TextBox" & (i - 1) * 3 + j).BackColor = &HFFFFFF
     Next j
   Next i
   UserForm1.Controls("TextBox11") = "0"
   UserForm1.Controls("TextBox12") = "0"
   UserForm1.Controls("TextBox13") = "0"
   UserForm1.Controls("TextBox14") = "0"
   UserForm1.Controls("TextBox10") = "Click Play To Start"
End Sub
```

FIGURE 2.20   InitFormFirst.

Although we have defined defaults for the textbox fields that track the scores, it is necessary to reset them at the end of each game so we can play a new game—the default only works once when we launch the program.

Let me explain how the

*UserForm1.Controls("TextBox" & (i − 1) * 3 + j) = "" works.*

Notice that I have put it in a double for loop so that it repeats nine times.

By using the formula *(i − 1) * 3 + j* we are able to generate a number from 1 to 9.

This is an indirect way to write the nine variable names (*UserForm1.Controls.TextBox1*, ..., ..., ..., *UserForm1.Controls.TextBox9)* making the code much more compact.

Now that the form is visible, we need code to play the game.

Go back to the form and double-click on the "Play" button.

Enter the following code.

```
Private Sub CommandButton1_Click()
    UserForm1.Controls("TextBox10") = ""
    Call InitForm
    RandomValue = Int((9 * Rnd) + 1)
    If UserForm1.TextBox10 = "" Then
        If UserForm1.OptionButton1 = True Then
            UserForm1.Controls("TextBox" & RandomValue) = "O"
        End If
    End If
End Sub
```

FIGURE 2.21   CommandButton1.

InitForm is defined in Module1 and its main purpose is to turn all cells white and get rid of the noughts and crosses from the previous game. See code below.

The Random statement creates a random number from 1 to 9 and places a "O" in that cell. This is only used if the computer plays first. The subsequent moves by the computer require further sophistication and will be explained later.

```
Sub InitForm()
    Dim cCont As Control
    For i = 1 To 3
        For j = 1 To 3
            UserForm1.Controls("TextBox" & (i - 1) * 3 + j) = ""
            UserForm1.Controls("TextBox" & (i - 1) * 3 + j).BackColor = &HFFFFFF
        Next j
    Next i

End Sub
```

FIGURE 2.22   InitForm.

Playing the game involves entering a "O" (nought) or a "X" (cross) in any of the nine cells that are not already used.

For simplicity and pneumonic ease, the computer is always assumed to be playing "O" and the human user "X".

Now there is one more point to think about. Entering "X" requires a keystroke from the keyboard as well as a mouse movement to pick the right cell. Wouldn't it be nice to just use the mouse instead? The good news is this is not so difficult. All we need to do is create the code for a "double-click" for each of the nine TextBoxes as shown below:

```
Private Sub TextBox1_DblClick(ByVal Cancel As MSForms.ReturnBoolean)
If UserForm1.TextBox1 = "" Then
   If UserForm1.TextBox10 = "" Then
      UserForm1.TextBox1 = "X"
   End If
   Call TicTacToe
End If
End Sub
```

FIGURE 2.23   Code in TextBox1.

TextBox10 is the message bar—it is only populated when the game is won or drawn.

Hence this is checked before an "X" is placed in the required cell.

Tic Tac Toe is the program that has the rest of the logic.

This is executed every time a user double-clicks in the middle of a new game.

The code for this subroutine is below. We will dive into each aspect of this code:

- How do we maintain the score?
- How does the computer know which cells are still empty?
- How does the computer determine the best move?

The following lines are required so that they can be accessed from any function. If we do not do this, these variables are only visible in the function they are defined in.

```
Public WinTag As Variant
Public Factor(3) As Variant
Public XScore As Double
Public OScore As Double
```

Now let us write the main code where the scoring lines are highlighted.

```
Sub TicTacToe()
Dim sbox(3, 3)
' sbox stores the current value

' *** initialize

WinTag = Array(0, 30, 238, 506, 627, 935, 1001, 1495, 7429)

If UserForm1.Controls("TextBox10") <> "" Then
   UserForm1.Controls("TextBox10") = "Click Play to Start"

Else
   A = ExamineEachFormCell(EmptyX, EmptyY, EmptyCount, OScore, XScore)
   If (WinOrLoss(OScore) = 1) Or (WinOrLoss(XScore) = 1) Or (EmptyCount = 0) Then

   Else
      Call ComputerPlay(XScore, OScore, EmptyCount)
   End If
   If EmptyCount = 0 Then
      UserForm1.Controls("TextBox10") = "DRAW!!!!!!!"
      UserForm1.Controls("TextBox13") = UserForm1.Controls("TextBox13") + 1
      UserForm1.Controls("TextBox14") = UserForm1.Controls("TextBox14") + 1
   End If

End Sub
```

```
Function ExamineEachFormCell(EmptyX, EmptyY, EmptyCount, OScore, XScore)
   EmptyCount = NextEmptyFormCell(EmptyX, EmptyY, OScore, XScore)
   If WinOrLoss(OScore) = 1 Then
      UserForm1.Controls("TextBox10") = "The COMPUTER Wins!"
      UserForm1.Controls("TextBox11") = UserForm1.Controls("TextBox11") + 1
   End If

   If WinOrLoss(XScore) = 1 Then
      UserForm1.Controls("TextBox10") = "YOU WON! Congratulations!!!"
      UserForm1.Controls("TextBox12") = UserForm1.Controls("TextBox12") + 1
   End If
End Function
```

The computer figures out which cell is empty by reviewing each cell for a value. The function passes the number of empty cells back because this is used to know if the game is drawn. The coordinates of the next empty cell are also passed along for the computer to use to play its next move. If there are no more cells left, then the game cannot be played any more—hence drawn.

```
Function NextEmptyFormCell(ByRef EmptyX, EmptyY, OScore, XScore)
Dim Factor(3)
Factor(1) = Array(0, 2, 3, 5)
Factor(2) = Array(0, 7, 11, 13)
Factor(3) = Array(0, 17, 19, 23)
   OScore = 1
   XScore = 1
   EmptyCount = 0
   EmptyX = 0
   EmptyY = 0
   For i = 1 To 3
     For j = 1 To 3
       If UserForm1.Controls("TextBox" & (i - 1) * 3 + j) = "" Then
         EmptyCount = EmptyCount + 1
         EmptyX = i
         EmptyY = j
       Else
         If UserForm1.Controls("TextBox" & (i - 1) * 3 + j) = "X" Then
           XScore = XScore * Factor(i)(j)
         Else
           OScore = OScore * Factor(i)(j)
         End If
       End If
     Next j
   Next i
   NextEmptyFormCell = EmptyCount
End Function
```

FIGURE 2.24   Find Next Empty Cell.

Here is how the computer determines the best move:

First, the computer examines if the next move by itself will result in a win.

Second, the computer considers that if it cannot win, can it prevent its opponent from winning? if the next move by the opponent will result in a win, it tries to block it by placing a "O".

Third, if neither of these are possible, then it determines the best cell.

All the three steps are based upon the algorithmic score described in the next section.

WinTag(k) stores the winning scores that are compared to the score attained by filling in that cell. The Greatest Common Divisor (GCD) function returns the cell's assigned value if the cell is a winning cell. In Step 3, the GCD is greater than 1 if the cell value is a multiple of any of the eight WinTag(k) scores. A count is kept of how many scores the value of the cell is a multiple of. The higher the number, the better the choice of the cell.

| **STEP 1** | ```
Sub ComputerPlay(XScore, OScore, EmptyCount)
  Factor(1) = Array(0, 2, 3, 5)
  Factor(2) = Array(0, 7, 11, 13)
  Factor(3) = Array(0, 17, 19, 23)
  ComputerPlayed = False
  If Not ComputerPlayed Then
    For k = 1 To 8
      For i = 1 To 3
        For j = 1 To 3
          If UserForm1.Controls("TextBox" & (i - 1) * 3 + j) = "" Then
            If WorksheetFunction.Gcd(WinTag(k), Factor(i)(j ) * OScore) = WinTag(k) Then
              UserForm1.Controls("TextBox" & (i - 1) * 3 + j) = "O"
              ComputerPlayed = True
              k = 9
              i = 4
              Exit For
            End If
          End If


        Next
      Next
    Next
  End If
``` |
| **STEP 2** | ```
If Not ComputerPlayed Then
  For k = 1 To 8
    For i = 1 To 3
      For j = 1 To 3
        If UserForm1.Controls("TextBox" & (i - 1) * 3 + j) = "" Then
          If WorksheetFunction.Gcd(WinTag(k), Factor(i)(j) * XScore) = WinTag(k) Then
          'If Factor(i)(j) * XScore = WinTag(k) Then
            UserForm1.Controls("TextBox" & (i - 1) * 3 + j) = "O"
            ComputerPlayed = True
            k = 9
            i = 4
            Exit For
          End If
        End If
      Next
    Next
  Next
End If
``` |

FIGURE 2.25   Computer Play.

STEP 3

```
If Not ComputerPlayed Then
    Call FIndBestOption(OScore, Be stCell)
End If
A = ExamineEachFormCell(EmptyX, EmptyY, EmptyCount, OScore, XScore)
'EmptyCount = NextEmptyFormCell(EmptyX, EmptyY, OScore, XScore)
End Sub
Sub FIndBestOption(OScore, BestCell)
    Factor(1) = Array(0, 2, 3, 5)
    Factor(2) = Array(0, 7, 11, 13)
    Factor(3) = Array(0, 17, 19, 23)
    BestCell = 0
    MaxPossibility = 0
    For k = 1 To 8
        Possibility = 0
        For i = 1 To 3
            For j = 1 To 3
                If UserForm1.Controls("TextBox" & (i - 1) * 3 + j) = "" Then
                    If BestCell = 0 Then
                        BestCell = (i - 1) * 3 + j
                    End If
                    If WorksheetFunction.Gcd(WinTag(k), Factor(i)(j) * OScor e) > 1 Then
                        Possibility = Possibility + 1
                        If MaxPossibility < Possibility Then
                            MaxPossibility = Possibility
                            BestCell = (i - 1) * 3 + j
                        End If
                    End If
                End If

            Next
        Next
    Next
    If BestCell > 0 Then
        UserForm1.Controls("TextBox" & BestCell) = "O"
    End If
End Sub
```

FIGURE 2.25   Continued

2.5   UNDERSTANDING THE NEED FOR AN ALGORITHM

When playing Tic Tac Toe, we see the winning line pretty easily:

- Any row
- Any column
- Any diagonal

With the same symbol (noughts or crosses)

But the computer cannot see the pattern that easily.

We already have a defined way to identify each of the nine cells in the game.

This is by the use of a row number (1–3) and a column number (1–3).

And we already know how to figure out the exact placement of noughts and crosses on the board.

So how can we use this information to identify a winning row? And what if there is no win but a draw?

This identifies a problem and the solution to this problem is an algorithm.

Here is the problem, written in somewhat mathematical terms:

- How can we define a function so that by executing this function on a set of any three rows, the result represents a "Win"?

At this point we are clear that this requires the assignment of a unique number to each cell.

See figure below.

1	2	3
4	5	6
7	8	9

FIGURE 2.26   Unique number for each cell.

Suppose we assign a unique integer to each cell 1,2,3…9.
We know that the following are winning combinations:

- Rows
  - 1,2,3
  - 4,5,6
  - 7,8,9
- Columns
  - 1,4,7
  - 2,5,8
  - 3,6,9
- Diagonals
  - 1,5,9
  - 3,5,7

One possible algorithm is to check the cells for this pattern. That would require a longish if statement nest is like the one below:

```
If Cell 1 = "X"
      If Cell2 = "X"
         If Cell3 = "X"
              XScore = Win
         End If
```

```
            End If
        Else If Cell 4 = "X"
            If Cell5 = "X"
                If Cell6 = "X"
                    XScore = Win
                End If
            End If
        :
        :
        End If
```

This would be just like the rudimentary 16-line code we reviewed at the beginning of this chapter that had several flaws such as being too long and not easily extensible for a matrix of order greater than 3.

Wouldn't it be nice to just apply one function to the cell values that tells us this is a Win for someone? This would potentially reduce the size of the code to one line, somewhat like this:

$$Function(X) = Win$$

Knowing that we can do any operation on the cells, we can experiment with a few choices.

Let's say we add them up.

			15
1	2	3	6
4	5	6	15
7	8	9	22
12	15	18	15

FIGURE 2.27   Unique totals.

The row totals are in yellow, column totals in blue, and diagonal totals in green.

This scheme would not work because the sums are not unique.

If they are not unique, you would not know what combination caused the win, simply by looking at the score.

A clever way of determining this is to assign prime numbers to each cell. Prime numbers have the unique property of having only two factors—1 and the number itself. Hence if we were to multiply the numbers in a row, column, or diagonal, they will always yield a unique value.

This is what an algorithm is—a clever, repeatable, and predictable way to perform a task in a program.

The magic square above now looks something like this:

			935
2	3	5	30
7	11	13	1001
17	19	23	7429
238	627	1495	506

FIGURE 2.28   Magic square.

Notice that each product is unique and can be easily identified as a winning number.

Here is the code to create the product for each row, which we call a "score". If a cell is not filled in, we assume that its value is 1, so that multiplying it has a neutral effect (any number multiplied by 1 is the number itself). Or, as in the code below, just do not multiply the value of that cell at all.

```
Function NextEmptyFormCell(ByRef, XScore)
Dim Factor(3)
Factor(1) = Array(0, 2, 3, 5)
Factor(2) = Array(0, 7, 11, 13)
Factor(3) = Array(0, 17, 19, 23)
   XScore = 1
   For i = 1 To 3
    For j = 1 To 3
        If UserForm1.Controls("TextBox" & (i - 1) * 3 + j) = "X" Then
           XScore = XScore * Factor(i)(j)
        End If
    Next j
   Next i
End Function
```

FIGURE 2.29   Next Empty Form Cell.

As far as possible, you would want to avoid checking specific values in an if statement—then this becomes a long, uncontrollable chain, as shown above.

One clever way is to divide the score by one of the eight "winning" products (shown in color in the square above). If the remainder is 0, then the score is a winner. Notice that this method achieves a huge simplification—you no longer have to check each triplet of cells. You can multiply all of them, and check for the remainder after dividing by each winning product. If the remainder is 0, then surely it has one of the winning combinations.

Here is the code that checks this in your program:

The variable WinOrLoss is 1 for a win.

```
Function WinOrLoss(ByVal Score As Double)
    WinOrLoss = 0
    Dim WinTag
    WinTag = Array(0, 30, 238, 506, 627, 935, 1001, 1495, 7429)
    For i = 1 To 8
        If Score > 0 Then
            If Score Mod WinTag(i) = 0 Then
                WinOrLoss = 1
            End If
        End If
    Next i
End Function
```

FIGURE 2.30   Win or loss.

⋮
⋮

2.6   HOW TO TEST DRIVE YOUR NEW CREATION

So far you have just run the program and expected it to work perfectly. In reality, that is never the case. An average programmer runs and reruns a program at least a 100 times. There is a tool in excel that allows you to do just this—run your program in a controlled fashion. Without this tool, running a program is like driving a car without brakes. If it is a perfect self-driving car, then you do not need to worry—it will drive itself.

But even a self-driving car needs human intervention for certain situations. So, just as you need to learn how to use the brakes, steering wheel, and accelerator for a car, you need to learn how to start, stop, examine, restart, and fix your code without feeling intimidated.

This leads us to a discussion on the debugger.

This is a tool that allows you to test your code and examine the values of the variables as they change through the program execution. You can pause anywhere and abandon the test at any time.

Step 1 is to decide which program you are going to run and place the cursor anywhere inside it. You would usually start with the very first program, that is typically the "launcher" for the rest of the code. In our case of the Tic Tac Toe, this must be the Subroutine called InitFormFirst. But that is only when you run it for the first time. There are several execution points, as you have seen—double-clicking on a cell, clicking on the "Play" button, etc.

One essential step in car driving is knowing your brakes—almost more important than knowing how to start. Similarly, you can stop the program on any executable line (an executable line is a line that has an action rather than a definition, such as a Dim statement).

Setting up any line to stop just requires double-clicking. When you do that, it is technically called "setting a break point". After setting it, if you change your mind, just double-click again and the break point goes away. You can also use the menu to turn the break point on or off. This is the option in the menu called "Toggle Breakpoint". Note that there are a few other features as well in the menu, which we will not go into in this chapter.

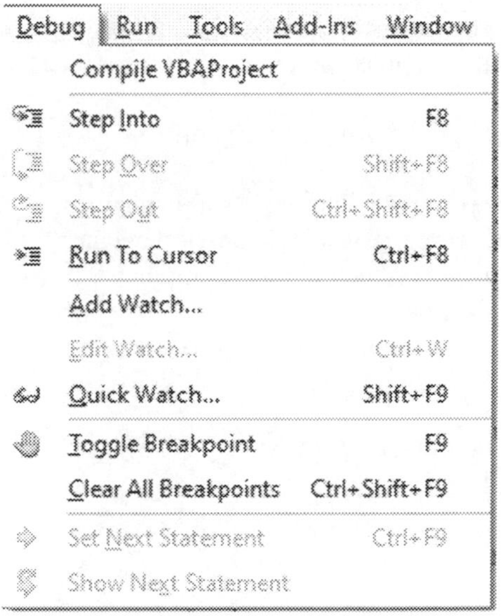
Debug
Run
Tools
Add-Ins
Window
Compile VBAProject
Step Into F8
Step Over Shift+F8
Step Out Ctrl+Shift+F8
Run To Cursor Ctrl+F8
Add Watch...
Edit Watch... Ctrl+W
Quick Watch... Shift+F9
Toggle Breakpoint F9
Clear All Breakpoints Ctrl+Shift+F9
Set Next Statement Ctrl+F9
Show Next Statement

FIGURE 2.31 Toggle Breakpoint.

Once you run the program and it stops at a break point, you can see the value of any variable in that function by simply hovering over the variable. See this example in Figure 2.32, where I stopped the code at the highlighted line. By hovering over the variable "OScore" we can see its value is 0 at this point.

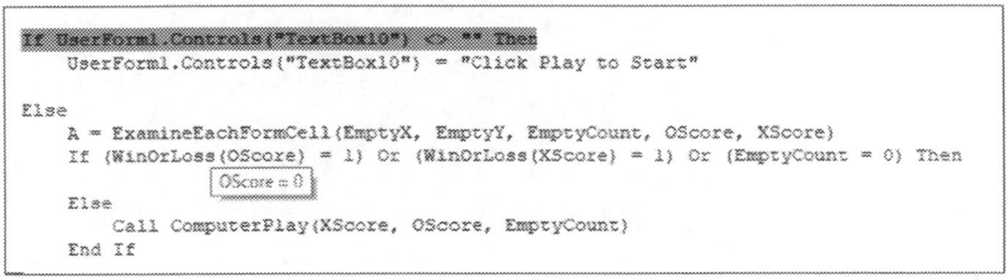
If UserForm1.Controls("TextBox10") <> "" Then
UserForm1.Controls("TextBox10") = "Click Play to Start"
Else
A = ExamineEachFormCell(EmptyX, EmptyY, EmptyCount, OScore, XScore)
If (WinOrLoss(OScore) = 1) Or (WinOrLoss(XScore) = 1) Or (EmptyCount = 0) Then
OScore = 0
Else
Call ComputerPlay(XScore, OScore, EmptyCount)
End If

FIGURE 2.32 Stopping Code.

2.7   CONCLUSION

Why Tic Tac Toe?

This is a program that has many qualities I wanted to highlight.

- The concept of an algorithm
- The iteration concept
- The selection concept
- The gamification of a process
- The introduction to various components of a user interface

Just to recap the algorithms we used in this game:

- Transferring the row and column to a single number
- Identifying if a "winning" row, column, or diagonal is formed
- Identifying the next best move for the computer

You also learnt the following concepts in this chapter:

- Using a function
- Declaration using PUBLIC
- How to build a Form
- Debugging
- If statements
- For statements

There is a glossary at the end of the book with these terms explained. Remember, you always have an online reference for the VBA language that you can consult—it is free and the link is provided in the "References" chapter at the end.

If you have built this already following the instructions I have described, you might like to extend your learning further.

Here is a problem for you. How can you extend this game to a 16 square (4 by 4) matrix?

3 Explore Your Deductive Logic
Solve a Sudoku Forever

The concept of Sudoku is attributed to Euler who lived in the 18th century and was responsible for famous mathematical inventions, including the constant *e* which is named after him. He solved the famous Basel problem and was responsible for defining a function with the term f(x) and developing the Power series:

$$e^x = \sum_{n=0}^{\infty} \frac{x^n}{n!} = \lim_{n \to \infty} \left(\frac{1}{0!} + \frac{x}{1!} + \frac{x^2}{2!} + \cdots + \frac{x^n}{n!} \right)$$

Sudoku is based on the concept of a Latin square that Euler discovered—an N by N matrix that has exactly one occurrence of N symbols in any row or column, an example with A, B, C below.

A	B	C
C	A	B
B	C	A

The aim of Sudoku is to place the digits 1 to 9 in a 9 by 9 grid so that each digit appears exactly once in each row, each column, and each of the nine 3 by 3 sub-grids in the 9 by 9 grid.

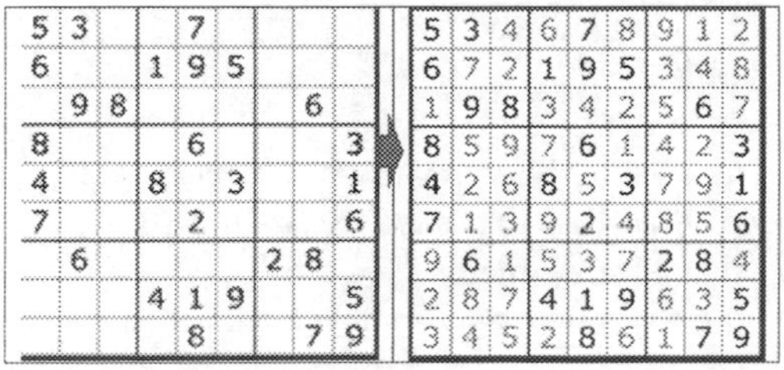

FIGURE 3.1 Sudoku.

DOI: 10.1201/9781003214335-4

The example above had only 30 of the 81 cells filled in and the objective of the Sudoku puzzle is to fill them all in.

Getting the correct number to fill in an empty cell can be hard but very addictive and fulfilling. After this puzzle exploded in popularity in 2005, most newspapers and magazines feature this puzzle and some grade it according to their level of difficulty. The popular belief is that the first Sudoku puzzle appeared in Japan in 1984, which explains its Japanese name. Sudoku is a shortened version of a Japanese expression, "Suji wa dokushin ni kagiru", which means the digits are limited to one occurrence.

In this chapter we are going to discuss the art of building algorithms to solve Sudoku puzzles using a macro.

We are not going to spend a lot of time on developing a nice user interface—you can do that on your own with the skills you have learnt in Chapter 2. Instead, we are going to focus on the logic of solving the puzzle and get inspired by the various techniques that can be implemented to solve them using a program.

You might be thinking, where is the fun of solving a puzzle like Sudoku if the program is going to solve it? We will discuss how you can use a combination of computer and human efforts to solve such a puzzle, so that the control still remains on the user on how much of the puzzle the user wants to solve oneself! Perhaps you got badly stuck with only five numbers to go? Perhaps you just want one more number? You can do that using code in the program that specifically stops or pauses in order to allow the user to exercise their brain!

The discussion starts with a simple user interface. Since this is played on a 9 by 9 grid, that is what we will do first.

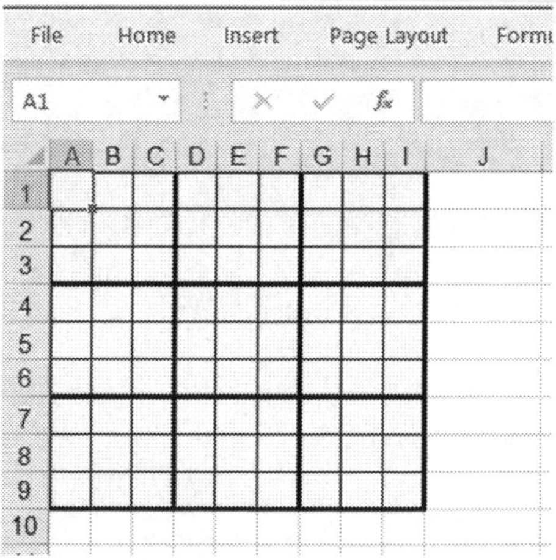

FIGURE 3.2   9 by 9 matrix.

We have now defined a 9 by 9 matrix as shown in the yellow highlighted area in our spreadsheet above. Note that I reduced the row and column widths so that they appear more like the real puzzle squares.

Each cell has an address. Since my cursor is on the first row and first column, the address being shown here is A1. In the program we will refer to each as *Cell(row, column)* where row and column vary from 1 to 9.

If you have solved Sudoku puzzles, you know that the most important thing to consider when you are looking to fill an empty cell is what it cannot be—each column, row, and 3 by 3 grid can have the numbers 1 to 9 only once. Hence, for each cell in the 9 by 9 grid that already has a value, it provides an exclusion for the row, column, and 3 by 3 grid that this cell identifies with.

Hence the program needs to keep track of these exclusions. We store these in a structure called "Array". An array is a way of storing variables so that we can refer to them using rows and columns. We call this array a "cantbelist" to store each of the numbers that it cannot be. We need three dimensions to store this—the row and the column to refer to which cell in the 9 by 9 grid we are talking about are two of them. The third dimension is the number that cell can't be. Let's take the example in Figure 3.3 to illustrate this:

COLUMN	1	2	3	4	5	6	7	8	9
1	7	3			2		4	5	
2	5		2	3	4	7			6
3			4				3	7	2
4	1	5	6	4	9	2	7	8	3
5	4	9	8		7	3		2	5
6	3	2	7		8				4
7		4	3	7			2		
8	2		5	9	1	4		3	7
9		7		2	3		5	4	

ROW

FIGURE 3.3   Developing cant be list.

Column 1 already has 1,2,3,4,5 and 7.

Hence, the "cantbelist" for all cells in column 1 must contain these numbers. So in column 1 we see three cells that are empty: (3,1) (7,1), and (9,1). The table below shows this information as array values.

Cell reference	Array reference	Value	Cell reference	Array reference	Value
(3,1)	cantbelist(3,1,1)	1	(7,1)	cantbelist(7,1,1)	1
(3,1)	cantbelist(3,1,2)	2	(7,1)	cantbelist(7,1,2)	2
(3,1)	cantbelist(3,1,3)	3	(7,1)	cantbelist(7,1,3)	3
(3,1)	cantbelist(3,1,4)	4	(7,1)	cantbelist(7,1,4)	4
(3,1)	cantbelist(3,1,5)	5	(7,1)	cantbelist(7,1,5)	5
(3,1)	cantbelist(3,1,6)	7	(7,1)	cantbelist(7,1,6)	7
(3,1)	cantbelist(3,1,7)	blank	(7,1)	cantbelist(7,1,7)	blank
(3,1)	cantbelist(3,1,8)	blank	(7,1)	cantbelist(7,1,8)	blank
(3,1)	cantbelist(3,1,9)	blank	(7,1)	cantbclist(7,1,9)	blank

Cell reference	Array reference	Value
(9,1)	cantbelist(9,1,1)	1
(9,1)	cantbelist(9,1,2)	2
(9,1)	cantbelist(9,1,3)	3
(9,1)	cantbelist(9,1,4)	4
(9,1)	cantbelist(9,1,5)	5
(9,1)	cantbelist(9,1,6)	7
(9,1)	cantbelist(9,1,7)	blank
(9,1)	cantbelist(9,1,8)	blank
(9,1)	cantbelist(9,1,9)	blank

Note that if we had two more numbers in the "cantbelist" array, we would be able to complete the cell.

This is the basic algorithm we need to solve for all the missing cells. As we look at every row, column, and 3 by 3 grid, we keep building the "cantbelist" since each cell may be influenced by the row, column, or 3 by 3 grid that it belongs to. As we build this, we stop when there is only one out of nine items left in the "cantbelist". This, therefore, must be the missing number!

This is how a human user solves the puzzle as well. The difference in using a computer is as follows:

- The computer can do it a lot faster.
- There are no chance of making mistakes.
- Computer can perform this task multiple times to refine the search for the missing number, since the discovery of one cell increases the entries in the "cantbelist" for other cells, thus improving the chances of finding missing numbers.

3.1   THE BASIC CODE FOR SOLVING A SUDOKU

Here is how the basic code can be written:

STEP 1	*Define the variables, initialize the cantbelist to 0 and set up the structure for building cantbelist.*
	We use variable "sbox" to store the current value of each cell in the 9 by 9 grid.
	Row is i, column is j.
	
	Public cantbelist() As Integer
	Public sbox(9, 9)
	
	For i = 1 To 9
	    For j = 1 To 9
	        sbox(i, j) = Cells(i, j)
	    Next j
	Next i

| **STEP 1 continued** | ```
For i = 1 To 9
  For j = 1 To 9
    For k = 1 To 9
      cantbelist(i, j, k) = 0
    Next k
  Next j
Next I

For i = 1 To 9
  For j = 1 To 9
  :
  : {Compare each cell sbox(I,j) with every **column**, building the cantbelist (Step 2)}
  :
  : {Compare each cell sbox(I,j) with every **row**, building the cantbelist (Step 3)}
  :
  : {Compare each cell sbox(I,j) with every **3 by 3 grid**, building the cantbelist (Step 4)}
  :
    Next j
  Next i
``` |
| **STEP 2** | *Check all columns.*<br>*The reason we need two variables for column is because to build up the cantbelist for each cell in the nine columns, you have to look at all the nine columns, hence need to repeat this $9 \times 9 = 81$ times. The function NextEmptyLocation simply finds the next empty value of the nine possible values for a cell in cantbelist. Note also the use of the variable "foundincantbelist". Initially set to 0, it gets set to 1 as soon as a match is found. This helps with avoiding redundant information by checking that the value of "foundincantbelist" is 1 before adding the number to cantbelist.*<br><br>```
For k = 1 To 9
  If j <> k Then
    If sbox(i, k) > 0 Then
      foundincantbelist = 0
      For kk = 1 To 9
        If sbox(i, k) = cantbelist(i, j, kk) Then foundincantbelist = 1
      Next kk
      If foundincantbelist = 0 Then
        cantbelist(i, j, NextEmptyLocation(i, j)) = sbox(i, k)
      End If
    End IF
  End If
Next k
:
:
Function NextEmptyLocation(ByVal i, j)
  For n = 1 To 9
  If cantbelist(i, j, n) = 0 Then
  NextEmptyLocation = n
  n = 9
  End If
  Next n
End Function
``` |

STEP 3	*Check all rows.*
	
	For k = 1 To 9
	  If i <> k Then
	    ' For m = 1 To 9
	    If sbox(k, j) > 0 Then
	      foundincantbelist = 0
	      For kk = 1 To 9
	        If sbox(k, j) = cantbelist(i, j, kk) Then foundincantbelist = 1
	      Next kk
	        If foundincantbelist = 0 Then
	          cantbelist(i, j, NextEmptyLocation(i, j)) = sbox(k, j)
	        End If
	      End If
	      ' Next m
	    End If
	  Next k:
	  :
	Next i

STEP 4	*Now we need to examine each cell in the 3 by 3 matrix this cell belongs to. The algorithm used to find the row and column values for the 3 by 3 grid is very simple. Both for row and column, the technique is to find the closest multiple of 3 and then add 1, 2, and 3 to it. The "int" function helps with this by removing the decimals. For example, the multiple of 3 closest to 7 is 6. You can get that by running this formula:*
	*Int((i - 1) / 3) * 3 where i is 7.*
	    For k = 1 To 3
	      n = Int((i - 1) / 3) * 3 + k
	      For l = 1 To 3
	        p = Int((j - 1) / 3) * 3 + l
	        If (l = n And j = p) Then
	          m = m '(do nothing)
	        Else
	          If sbox(n, p) <> "" Then
	            foundincantbelist = 0
	            For kk = 1 To 9
	            If sbox(n, p) = cantbelist(i, j, kk) Then foundincantbelist = 1
	            Next kk
	            If foundincantbelist = 0 Then
	            cantbelist(i, j, NextEmptyLocation(i, j)) = sbox(n, p)
	            End If
	          End If
	        End If
	      Next l
	    Next k

Now that the "cantbelist" is built, we can simply check its contents. Any empty cell with eight values (from 1 to 9) in "cantbelist" must be assigned the ninth digit. This next code does exactly that.

```
STEP 5

    For i = 1 To 9
      For j = 1 To 9
        If sbox(i, j) = "" Then
            whatisthisnumber = 0
            For k = 1 To 9
            If cantbelist(i, j, k) > 0 Then
                howmanycantbe = k
                whatisthisnumber = whatisthisnumber + cantbelist(i, j, k)
            End If
            Next k
              If howmanycantbe = 8 Then
                 sbox(i, j) = 45 - whatisthisnumber
                 Cells(i, j) = sbox(i, j)
                 Call updatecantbelist(sbox(i, j), i, j)
              End If
            End If
          Next j
      Next i
```

3.2   ITERATIVE BUILD OF CANTBELIST

Now let's talk about iterations. As soon as you find a missing cell, there is a need to update the cantbelist. This is why we have the call to updatecantbelist—which is made up of the same steps as steps 2 to 4. (Full code is in the back of this book.) But if cantbelist has changed, you need to reexamine cantbelist because now there may be more cells reaching the threshold of eight "cantbelist" entries. This is why we need to go through this code again and again. You can control how many times you want to repeat. In the simplest way, you can just repeat it ten times. In order to repeat ten times, you will need extra lines of code in step 5, shown below in red. Note the use of the "inputbox" statement. This allows us to ask the user if the user wants to go ahead with the next iteration. It will perform the next iteration only if the user answers "Y" for yes. This will allow the user to get a few numbers at a time, but not all of them, so that the pleasure of solving the puzzle can be retained a bit longer.

```
STEP 5

    For Iteration = 1 To 10
    For i = 1 To 9
      For j = 1 To 9
        If sbox(i, j) = "" Then
            whatisthisnumber = 0
            For k = 1 To 9
            If cantbelist(i, j, k) > 0 Then
                howmanycantbe = k
                whatisthisnumber = whatisthisnumber + cantbelist(i, j, k)
            End If
```

STEP 5 continued	Next k
	  If howmanycantbe = 8 Then
	    sbox(i, j) = 45 - whatisthisnumber
	    Cells(i, j) = sbox(i, j)
	    Call updatecantbelist(sbox(i, j), i, j)
	  End If
	  End If
	 Next j
	Next i
	continue = InputBox("Iteration" & Iteration & "complete. Continue?Y/N")
	If continue <> "Y" Then End
	Next Iteration

3.3 ALGORITHMS THAT A COMPUTER CAN SOLVE BETTER THAN HUMANS

So far whatever we have done using code is doable comfortably by a human—it just takes longer but the logic is reasonably straightforward. If you have done serious Sudoku, you would have come across some puzzles that are extremely hard. You may be staring at the puzzle for hours until the light fades and you realize that it is time to turn on the table lamp! These are the types of puzzles that need us to venture into further algorithms without which we just cannot solve the puzzle completely.

One such algorithm is to find 8 cells in a row, column, or 3 by 3 grid that is definitely not a certain number from 1 to 9. If that is the case, then the ninth cell must be that number. This is the principle behind the code in steps 6, 7, and 8.

STEP 6	*check all columns row by row for all numbers 1–9 (putnumber)*
	if the number is invalid in 8 of the nine cells in the same row, then the number must belong to the ninth cell (empty, of course).
	For putnumber = 1 to 9
	  For i = 1 To 9
	    numberfound = 0
	if the number we are searching for (putnumber) already exists in this row, then no need to proceed. This is controlled through the value of variable numberfound, by setting it to "1" and ignoring it for the rest of the code if this number already exists
	    For j = 1 To 9
	      If sbox(i, j) = putnumber Then numberfound = 1
	    Next j
	"notahome" is a variable that is used to flag an empty cell if the cantbelist array contains the number we are searching for (putnumber) number we are searching for (putnumber) because this cell is "not a home" for it. A count is kept in the variable "notahomecount" to determine how many cells in this row have banished this number. This is because if eight cells have, then the ninth cell must be this number.
	    If numberfound = 0 Then
	      notahomecount = 0

STEP 6 continued	```
For j = 1 To 9
notahome = 0
If sbox(i, j) <> "" Then notahome = 1
For k = 1 To 9
If cantbelist(i, j, k) = putnumber Then notahome = 1
Next k
If notahome = 1 Then
notahomecount = notahomecount + 1
Else
home = j
End If
Next j
If notahomecount = 8 Then
sbox(i, home) = putnumber
``` ***Remember to update cantbelist since we uncovered a new empty cell!*** ```
Call updatecantbelist(putnumber, i, home)
Cells(i, home) = sbox(i, home)
End If
End If
Next i
:
:
Next putnumber
``
STEP 7	***Now check all rows column by column for all numbers 1–9 (putnumber) if the number is invalid in eight of the nine cells in the same row, then the number must belong to the ninth cell (empty, of course).*** ```
For putnumber = 1 to 9
:
:
   For j = 1 To 9
      numberfound = 0

      For i = 1 To 9
         If sbox(i, j) = putnumber Then numberfound = 1
      Next i

   If numberfound = 0 Then
      notahomecount = 0
      For i = 1 To 9
         notahome = 0
         If sbox(i, j) <> "" Then notahome = 1
         For k = 1 To 9
            If cantbelist(i, j, k) = putnumber Then notahome = 1
         Next k
         If notahome = 1 Then
            notahomecount = notahomecount + 1
``` |
```

| **STEP 7 continued** | ```
        Else
           home = i
        End If
     Next i
     If notahomecount = 8 Then
           sbox(home, j) = putnumber
           Call updatecantbelist(putnumber, home, j)
           Cells(home, j) = sbox(home, j)
        End If
     End If
  Next j
  :
  :
Next putnumber
``` |
| **STEP 8** | *Now check all cells in the 3 by 3 grid for all numbers 1–9 (putnumber)*<br>*if the number is invalid in eight of the nine cells in the same row, then the number*<br>*must belong to the ninth cell (empty, of course).*<br><br>```
For putnumber = 1 to 9
  :
  :

  For i = 1 To 3
  For j = 1 To 3
     For k = 1 To 3
        n = Int((i - 1) / 3) * 3 + k
     For l = 1 To 3
        p = Int((j - 1) / 3) * 3 + l
        numberfound = 0
        If sbox(n, p) = putnumber Then numberfound = 1
     Next l
  Next k

  If numberfound = 0 Then
     notahomecount = 0
     For k = 1 To 3
        n = Int((i - 1) / 3) * 3 + k
        For l = 1 To 3
           p = Int((j - 1) / 3) * 3 + l
           notahome = 0
           If sbox(n, p) <> "" Then notahome = 1
           For kk = 1 To 9
              If cantbelist(n, p, kk) = putnumber Then notahome = 1
           Next kk
           If notahome = 1 Then
              notahomecount = notahomecount + 1
           Else
              homerow = n
              homecol = p
           End If
``` |

<table>
<tr><td rowspan="13" style="writing-mode: vertical-rl">STEP 8 continued</td><td>Next l</td></tr>
</table>

```
                Next l
                Next k
           If notahomecount − 8 Then
                sbox(homerow, homecol) = putnumber
                Call updatecantbelist(putnumber, homerow, homecol)
                Cells(homerow, homecol) = sbox(homerow, homecol)
           End If
           End If
           Next j
      Next i
      Next putnumber
```

(STEP 8 continued)

3.4   3 BY 3 GRID INTERACTION

The next advanced algorithm we are going to look at explores the interaction between two 3 by 3 grids that are adjacent to each other. If two adjacent 3 by 3 grids share the same rows, and a certain number can only be in two of the three rows in the 3 by 3 grid and the adjacent 3 by 3 grid can also only have it in the same two of the three rows, then the third 3 by 3 grid adjacent to it and sharing the same rows cannot have that number in the same two rows. See example below.

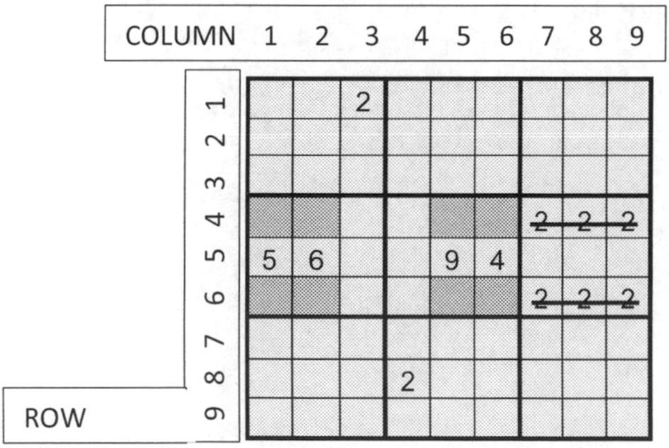

FIGURE 3.4   Interaction between grids.

The code in steps 9 and 10 executes this algorithm, but with a slight twist. Instead of working on the cells that share the same rows for a specific number (2 in the example above), the code works on the row that does not have this number. This is easier because we already have a matrix that stores what each cell is NOT (the "cantbelist").

The principle here is to compare the cell with each of the nine numbers, one grid at a time. If the number is found in cantbelist for a cell, or the cell is occupied by a number that is not the same as the number being searched, then a count is kept to see how many cells are there of this kind in that row. If there are 3, then it is a candidate, less than 3 does not qualify hence count is reset to zero for that grid. If the count is 6 for that row, this means there are two out of the three adjacent grids that cannot have this number. Hence the third grid included in this row must have this number. Therefore, the other rows in this third grid cannot have this number— these are then added to the cantbelist.

```
For putnumber = 1 to 9
  :

  :

  ' *** algorithm to refine cantbelist based on one row of 3 by 3 grid
For i = 1 To 9
   middlerowcount(i) = 0
Next i

   For i = 1 To 9 Step 3
      For j = 1 To 9 Step 3
         For k = 1 To 3
         n = Int((i - 1) / 3) * 3 + k
         triocount = 0
         For l = 1 To 3
            p = Int((j - 1) / 3) * 3 + l
               If (sbox(n, p) <> putnumber And sbox(n, p) <> "") Or
               findincantbelist(putnumber, n, p) = 1 Then
               middlerowcount(n) = middlerowcount(n) + 1
               triocount = triocount + 1

            End If
         Next l
         If triocount < 3 Then
            middlerowcount(n) = middlerowcount(n) - triocount
            savedcolumn(n) = p
         End If
      Next k
   Next j
Next i
For i = 1 To 9
   If middlerowcount(i) = 6 Then
      a = i Mod 3
      If a = 0 Then
         savedrow1 = i - 2
         savedrow2 = i - 1
      Else
      If a = 1 Then
         savedrow1 = i + 1
         savedrow2 = i + 2
      Else
```

STEP 9

| **STEP 9 continued** | ```
          savedrow1 = i - 1
          savedrow2 = i + 1
      End If
      End If

      Call addtocantbelist(putnumber, savedrow1, savedcolumn(i))
      Call addtocantbelist(putnumber, savedrow1, savedcolumn(i) - 1)
      Call addtocantbelist(putnumber, savedrow1, savedcolumn(i) - 2)
      Call addtocantbelist(putnumber, savedrow2, savedcolumn(i))
      Call addtocantbelist(putnumber, savedrow2, savedcolumn(i) - 1)
      Call addtocantbelist(putnumber, savedrow2, savedcolumn(i) - 2)
    End If
  Next i
  :
  :
Next putnumber

Function findincantbelist(thisnumber, thisrow, thiscolumn)
    findincantbelist = 0
    For i = 1 To 8
      If cantbelist(thisrow, thiscolumn, i) <> 0 Then
        If cantbelist(thisrow, thiscolumn, i) = thisnumber Then
            findincantbelist = 1
        End If
``` |
| **STEP 9** | ```
      End If
    Next i

End Function
``` |
| **STEP 10** | *This step is almost a repeat of the step 9, but now for columns. In step 9 we checked the adjacency of grids horizontally. The same needs to be done vertically to get the exclusion list prepared for the correct columns. The principle here is the same—to compare the cell with each of the nine numbers, one grid at a time. If the number is found in cantbelist for a cell, or the cell is occupied by a number that is not the same as the number being searched, then a count is kept to see how many cells are there of this kind in that column. If there are 3, then it is a candidate, less than 3 does not qualify hence count is reset to zero for that grid. If the count is 6 for that column, this means there are two out of the three adjacent grids that cannot have this number. Hence the third grid included in this column must have this number. Therefore, the other columns in this third grid cannot have this number—these are then added to the cantbelist.*<br><br>```
For putnumber = 1 to 9
:
:
' *** algorithm to refine cantbelist based on one column of 3 by 3 grid
For i = 1 To 9
    middlecolumncount(i) = 0
``` |
```

STEP 10 continued

```
Next i
For i = 1 To 9 Step 3
  For j = 1 To 9 Step 3
    For k = 1 To 3
      ' n is column p is row
      n = Int((i - 1) / 3) * 3 + k
      triocount = 0
      For l = 1 To 3
        p = Int((j - 1) / 3) * 3 + l
          If (sbox(p, n) <> putnumber And sbox(p, n) <> "") Or
            findincantbelist(putnumber, p, n) = 1 Then
            middlecolumncount(n) = middlecolumncount(n) + 1
            triocount = triocount + 1
          End If
        Next l
        If triocount < 3 Then
          middlecolumncount(n) = middlecolumncount(n) - triocount
          savedrow(n) = p
        End If
      Next k
    Next j
  Next i
For i = 1 To 9
  If middlecolumncount(i) = 6 Then
    a = i Mod 3
      If a = 0 Then
        savedcolumn1 = i - 2
        savedcolumn2 = i - 1
      Else
      If a = 1 Then
        savedcolumn1 = i + 1
        savedcolumn2 = i + 2
      Else
        savedcolumn1 = i - 1
        savedcolumn2 = i + 1
      End If
      End If
      Call addtocantbelist(putnumber, savedrow(i), savedcolumn1)
      Call addtocantbelist(putnumber, savedrow(i) - 1, savedcolumn1)
      Call addtocantbelist(putnumber, savedrow(i) - 2, savedcolumn1)
      Call addtocantbelist(putnumber, savedrow(i), savedcolumn2)
      Call addtocantbelist(putnumber, savedrow(i) - 1, savedcolumn2)
      Call addtocantbelist(putnumber, savedrow(i) - 2, savedcolumn2)
    End If
Next i
:
:
Next putnumber
```

You might be wondering, how many more algorithms can we think of to refine the answers for a Sudoku puzzle? The answer is as difficult as the question "How many bugs are there in my program?" It is what mathematicians call an "indeterminate" number—it is not possible to calculate it. I guess there is no algorithm to calculate how many algorithms are possible to solve a problem—you only know the number of algorithms that have been discovered, similar to the number of bugs in a program that have been uncovered.

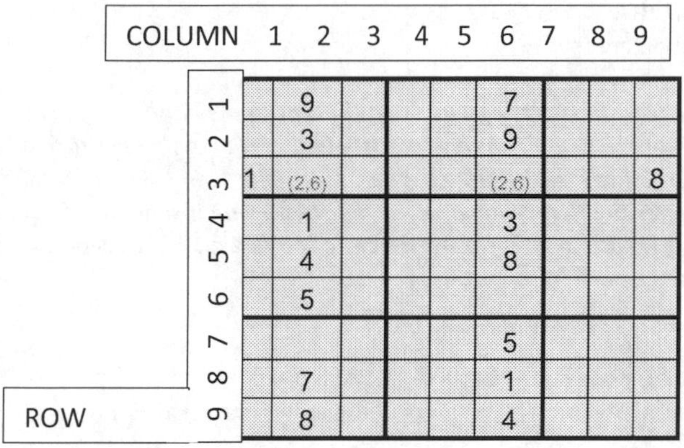

COLUMN	1	2	3	4	5	6	7	8	9
1		9				7			
2		3				9			
3	1 (2,6)				(2,6)			8	
4		1				3			
5		4				8			
6		5							
7						5			
8		7				1			
9		8				4			

ROW

FIGURE 3.5 Love-locked pair.

3.5 LOVE-LOCKED PAIR

The next algorithm I am going to discuss identifies a "pair"—to help you remember it, I will call it a "love-locked" pair. The point is that if two numbers are the only two possible solutions for two cells in a row, then those two numbers cannot be solutions for any other cells in the same row. Even though it may seem fairly obvious, it does need some smart manipulation of variables to execute it. In the example above, row 3 columns 2 and 6 have the same "love-locked" pair of numbers that will potentially fill them—2 and 6. But that means 2 and 6 cannot be anywhere else in the same row.

In the next few steps, I will explain how you can utilize this valuable insight in your algorithm.

STEP 11

The first step is to identify the candidates for each cell and store them away. In order to do this we count the number of items in our cantbelist array. Only those who have 7 are candidates.

```
For i = 1 To 9
  For j = 1 To 9
    cantbelistcount(i, j) = 0
    For k = 1 To 9
      If cantbelist(i, j, k) <> 0 Then
        cantbelistcount(i, j) = cantbelistcount(i, j) + 1
      End If
    Next k
```

<table>
<tr><td>

STEP 11 continued

</td><td>

Once identified, we store the two digits as a string in an array we call
putnumberpresent.

```
If sbox(i, j) = "" And cantbelistcount(i, j) = 7 Then
    putnumberpresent(i, j) = ""
    For putnumber = 1 To 9
        If findincantbelist(putnumber, i, j) = 0 Then
            putnumberpresent(i, j) = putnumberpresent(i, j) & putnumber
        End If
    Next putnumber
End If
```

Now we check the entire row and add the pair to the cantbelist for those cells. As
you see below, it is done in three parts—first part being from the first member of the
row to the cell before the first member of the pair (1 to k-1), the second from the cell
straight after the first member of the pair to the one just before the second member
of the pair (k+1 to i-1), the third from the cell just after the second member of the
pair to the last cell of the row (i+1 to 9).

```
For k = 1 To i - 1
    If putnumberpresent(k, j) <> "" And
        putnumberpresent(k, j) = putnumberpresent(i, j) Then
        For kk = 1 To k - 1
            Call addtocantbelist(Mid(putnumberpresent(k, j), 1, 1), kk, j)
            Call addtocantbelist(Mid(putnumberpresent(k, j), 2, 1), kk, j)
        Next kk
        For kk = k + 1 To i - 1
            Call addtocantbelist(Mid(putnumberpresent(k, j), 1, 1), kk, j)
            Call addtocantbelist(Mid(putnumberpresent(k, j), 2, 1), kk, j)
        Next kk
        For kk = i + 1 To 9
            Call addtocantbelist(Mid(putnumberpresent(k, j), 1, 1), kk, j)
            Call addtocantbelist(Mid(putnumberpresent(k, j), 2, 1), kk, j)
        Next kk
        Exit For
    End If
    Next k
Next j
Next i
```

</td></tr>
<tr><td>

STEP 12

</td><td>

The next step is to do the same for each column.

```
For i = 1 To 9
    For j = 1 To 9
        cantbelistcount(j, i) = 0
        For k = 1 To 9
            If cantbelist(j, i, k) <> 0 Then
                cantbelistcount(j, i) = cantbelistcount(j, i) + 1
            End If
```

</td></tr>
</table>

STEP 12 continued	Next k
	If sbox(j, i) = "" And cantbelistcount(j, i) = 7 Then
	  putnumberpresent(j, i) = ""
	  For putnumber = 1 To 9
	    If findincantbelist(putnumber, j, i) = 0 Then
	      putnumberpresent(j, i) = putnumberpresent(j, i) & putnumber
	    End If
	  Next putnumber
	End If
	For k = 1 To i - 1
	  If putnumberpresent(j, k) <> "" And
	  putnumberpresent(j, k) = putnumberpresent(j, i) Then
	  For kk = 1 To k - 1
	    Call addtocantbelist(Mid(putnumberpresent(j, k), 1, 1), j, kk)
	    Call addtocantbelist(Mid(putnumberpresent(j, k), 2, 1), j, kk)
	  Next kk
	  For kk = k + 1 To i - 1
	    Call addtocantbelist(Mid(putnumberpresent(j, k), 1, 1), j, kk)
	    Call addtocantbelist(Mid(putnumberpresent(j, k), 2, 1), j, kk)
	  Next kk
	  For kk = i + 1 To 9
	    Call addtocantbelist(Mid(putnumberpresent(j, k), 1, 1), j, kk)
	    Call addtocantbelist(Mid(putnumberpresent(j, k), 2, 1), j, kk)
	  Next kk
	  Exit For
	  End If
	  Next k
	  Next j
	Next i

STEP 13	*The final step is to do the same for each 3 by 3 grid. We do not need to create the putnumberpresent row again, since we have already built it. But it is a good idea to refresh this list each time the cantbelist is updated.*
	
	For i = 1 To 9 Step 3
	  For j = 1 To 9 Step 3
	    For k = 1 To 3
	      n = Int((i - 1) / 3) * 3 + k
	      For l = 1 To 3
	        p = Int((j - 1) / 3) * 3 + l
	        For ka = 1 To 3
	          na = Int((i - 1) / 3) * 3 + ka
	          For la = 1 To 3
	            pa = Int((j - 1) / 3) * 3 + la
	            If n <> na Or p <> pa Then
	              If putnumberpresent(n, p) <> "" And
	              putnumberpresent(n, p) = putnumberpresent(na, pa) Then

STEP 13 continued

```
                    For kb = 1 To 3
                        nb = Int((i - 1) / 3) * 3 + kb
                        For lb = 1 To 3
                            pb = Int((j - 1) / 3) * 3 + lb
                            If (nb = n And pb = p) Or (nb = na And pb = pa) Then
                            Else
                                Call addtocantbelist(Mid(putnumberpresent(n, p), 1, 1), nb, pb)
                                Call addtocantbelist(Mid(putnumberpresent(n, p), 2, 1), nb, pb)
                            End If
                        Next lb
                        Next kb
                        la = 4 'Exit For
                        ka = 4 'Exit For
                        l = 4 'Exit For
                        k = 4 'Exit For
                        End If
                    End If
                Next la
            Next ka
        Next l
    Next k
Next j
Next ii
```

This algorithm can be extended to work for not only a "love-locked pair" but also a trio (3), quartet (4), quintet (5), or sextet (6). The instructions become more complicated and the likelihood of finding such a case is progressively lower, as you advance in your goal of uncovering all the blank cells.

One other variation of this theme involves a slight redefinition of the love-locked pair. In the previous method, we saw that the candidates for the "love-locked pair" are those that have exactly the same two candidates in the same cell, row, or 3 by 3 grid. The same is true if exactly the same two numbers are the sole candidates for two different cells in the same row, column, or 3 by 3 grid. This is a slightly different situation where each "love-locked pair" cell can have more than two candidates. See example in Figure 3.6:

COLUMN	1	2	3	4	5	6	7	8	9
1			7	5			6	2	9
2		3							
3	4	(2,5,6)	9	1	3	7	8		
4		1							
5		4							
6	3	(5,7,9)	2	4	6		1	8	
7	9	(2,5,6)	1	3	4	8	7		
8	7			6	2	9	5		
9		8							

ROW

FIGURE 3.6   Second love-locked pair.

Just focusing on column 2, notice that 5 can be in rows 3, 6, or 7. But 2 and 6 can only be in rows 3 and 7. Since 5 has an alternate home and 2 and 6 don't, 5 can be eliminated from rows 3 and 7. This makes 5 a sole candidate for row 6.

The instructions for this method will be similar but slightly different from the previous "love-locked pair" scenario. Instead of looking for cells that have exactly seven members in their cantbelist in the same row, column, or 3 by 3 grid, we will need to look for two "putnumbers" that can occupy the same two cells. I have left it for the reader to figure this out.

3.6   THE GOLDEN TRIANGLE

The next algorithm we will discuss is the algorithm of the golden rectangle.

In the example below, 2 can only be in rows 2 and 8 for the green columns. This means 2 cannot be in the red cells in the rows 2 and 8 because the corners of the rectangle marked by the number (2) below have to be occupied with 2. This means we can remove 2 from the *cantbelist* for all the red cells.

COLUMN	1	2	3	4	5	6	7	8	9
ROW 1			1				5		
2			(2,6)				(2,3)		
3			3				4		
4			4				8		
5			5				9		
6			7				1		
7			8				6		
8			(2,6)				(2,3)		
9			9				7		

FIGURE 3.7   Golden rectangle.

The code below can be used to apply this logic.

The first step is to identify the corners of the rectangle and store them in an array. This array is called putnumberpresent below. The entire column is scanned for a candidate number (putnumber) and if the column contains exactly two cells that could be a home for this number, this column is remembered along with the two rows that could potentially be the two corners of the rectangle.

'*** algorithm to detect a golden rectangle

' Check each column and build putnumberpresent

For putnumber = 1 To 9
:

STEP 14 continued

```
For i = 1 To 9
  For j = 1 To 9
    putnumberpresent(i, j) = ""
  Next j
Next i

For i = 1 To 9
  ColumnCount = 0
  putnumberpresent(1, i) = ""
  lastcorner = ""
  For j = 1 To 9
    If sbox(j, i) = "" Then
      If findincantbelist(putnumber, j, i) = 0 Then
        lastcorner = lastcorner & j
        putnumberpresent(j, i) = lastcorner
        ColumnCount = ColumnCount + 1
      End If
    End If
  Next j
  If ColumnCount = 2 Then
  Else
    putnumberpresent(1, i) = "*"
  End If
Next i
  :
  :
```

STEP 15

The second step is to scan the putnumberpresent array to identify the other two corners. Once identified, all cells in the same two rows that the corners are in get the candidate number (putnumber) in each of their cantbelist (remember the array that stores what the cell cannot be?) except for the corners of the rectangle.
  :
  :

```
For i = 1 To 9
  For j = 1 To 9
    If putnumberpresent(1, j) <> "*" And sbox(i, j) = "" And
      putnumberpresent(i, j) <> "" Then
    For k = j To 9
      If putnumberpresent(i, k) = putnumberpresent(i, j) And k <> j And
        Len(putnumberpresent(i, j)) = 2 And putnumberpresent(1, k) <>
"*" Then
                    'column j,k and rows stored in putnumber are the rectangle
                    'all cells in the rows of the rectangle except the corners,
                    'should have putnumber in cantbelist
                    For kk = 1 To 9
                      If kk = j Or kk = k Then
                      Else
                        Call addtocantbelist(putnumber, Mid(putnumberpresent(i, j), 1,
1), kk)
```

STEP 15 continued	Call addtocantbelist(putnumber, Mid(putnumberpresent(i, j), 2, 1), kk)
	
	                                    End If
	                            Next kk
	                        End If
	                    Next k
	                End If
	            Next j
	        Next i
	:
	Next putnumber

Now that we have looked at the rectangle by scanning columns, the same needs to be done by scanning rows, as the results of the two scans can be different.

The following codes provide the two steps needed to complete this scan.

| **STEP 16** | *The first step is to identify the corners of the rectangle and store them in an array. This array is called putnumberpresent below. The entire row is scanned for a candidate number (putnumber) and if the row contains exactly two cells that could be a home for this number, this row is remembered along with the two columns that could potentially be the two corners of the rectangle.*<br><br>' algorithm for golden triangle continued<br>' Now Check each row and build putnumberpresent<br><br>```
For putnumber = 1 To 9
  For i = 1 To 9
    For j = 1 To 9
      putnumberpresent(i, j) = ""
    Next j
  Next i
  For i = 1 To 9
    RowCount = 0
    putnumberpresent(i, 1) = ""
    lastcorner = ""
    For j = 1 To 9
    If sbox(i, j) = "" Then
    If findincantbelist(putnumber, i, j) = 0 Then
      lastcorner = lastcorner & j
      putnumberpresent(i, j) = lastcorner
      RowCount = RowCount + 1
    End If
    End If
    Next j
    If RowCount = 2 Then
    Else
      putnumberpresent(i, 1) = "*"
    End If
  Next i
:
:
``` |
```

STEP 17

The second step is to scan the putnumberpresent array to identify the other two corners.
Once identified, all cells in the same two columns that the corners are in get the candidate number (putnumber) in each of their cantbelist (remember the array that stores what the cell cannot be?) except for the corners of the rectangle.
:
:

```
For i = 1 To 9
For j = 1 To 9
   If putnumberpresent(j, 1) <> "*" And sbox(j, i) = ""
      And putnumberpresent(j, i) <> "" Then
      For k = j To 9
         If putnumberpresent(k, i) = putnumberpresent(j, i) And k <> j
         And Len(putnumberpresent(j, i)) = 2 And putnumberpresent(1, k) <>
         "*" Then
         'row j,k and columns stored in putnumber are the rectangle
         'all cells in the columns of the rectangle except the corners,
         'should have putnumber in cantbelist
         For kk = 1 To 9
            If kk = j Or kk = k Then
            Else
               Call addtocantbelist(putnumber, kk, Mid(putnumberpresent(j,
               i), 1, 1))
               Call addtocantbelist(putnumber, kk, Mid(putnumberpresent(j,
               i), 2, 1))
            End If
         Next kk
         End If
      Next k
   End If
Next j
Next i
:
Next putnumber
```

There are two final algorithms I wanted to present before moving on to Chapter 4 on remote control.

3.7   THE POLYOMINO

The first one is called the algorithm of the polyomino. A polyomino is a two-dimensional figure that you can form by joining multiple squares. It is derived from the term domino—those little squares used in the domino game.

The second is the algorithm of the matching twin.

Here is how the first one works. In the diagram below, 2 is a candidate in exactly two cells in columns 2, 3, and 6. Notice how they form a closed pattern. The consequence of this pattern is that 2 can be eliminated from all cells in rows 3, 5, and 7 except for the corners of this pattern, marked with (2).

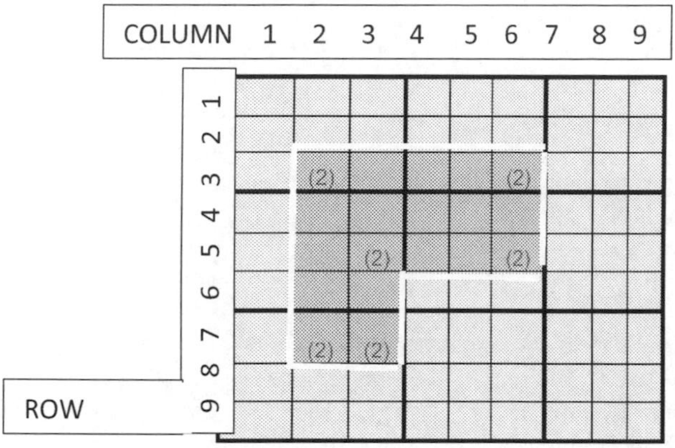

FIGURE 3.8   Polyomino.

The golden rectangle algorithm we discussed earlier has a step that identifies the first 2 corners of the rectangle. We can utilize this logic to extend the concept of the golden rectangle to a polyomino as shown above. If you recall, we start scanning from the left, to search for a column that has exactly two candidates for a certain "putnumber". Once we find a column that meets this criterion, we keep looking for more columns to the right that are similar. Then, we collect the row numbers for the candidate cells in all the columns found. If three columns are found, then there are six cells. If they contain only three unique row numbers, then this is a golden polyomino. (Fun fact: in the example above, it is an **enneadecamino** because it is made up of 19 squares.) Similarly, if four columns are found, there are eight cells—if these eight cells have only four unique row numbers, then this is also a golden polyomino. Note that the golden rectangle is a specific example of this situation where there are only two columns that meet this criterion and the four candidate cells have only three unique rows.

The codes that follow are the three steps to examine the 9 by 9 grid for a polyomino, collect the row numbers, and then use that information to update the relevant rows of cells with the number.

Note that this code is to scan the matrix *row by row* for columns that have the same possible number only in two out of nine rows. A similar piece of code is required to examine the matrix *column by column* for rows that have the same possible number only in two out of 9nine columns. This is a good exercise for you to solve.

Also, note also that the golden rectangle algorithm is a special case of a polyomino hence no longer required separately if you are implementing the algorithm of the polyomino.

The first step is to identify the corners of the polyomino and store them in an array. This array is called putnumberpresent below. The entire row is scanned for a candidate number (putnumber) and if the column contains exactly two cells that could be a home for this number, this column is remembered along with the two rows that could potentially be the two vertices of the polyomino.

STEP 18

```
'*** algorithm to detect a golden polyomino

' Check each column and build putnumberpresent
For putnumber = 1 To 9
   For i = 1 To 9
      PCol(i) = ""
   Next i
   ColCount = 0
   For i = 1 To 9
      ColumnCount = 0
      putnumberpresent(1, i) = ""
      lastcorner = ""
      For j = 1 To 9
         If sbox(j, i) = "" Then
            If findincantbelist(putnumber, j, i) = 0 Then
               lastcorner = lastcorner & j
               putnumberpresent(j, i) = lastcorner
               ColumnCount = ColumnCount + 1
            End If
         End If
      Next j
      If ColumnCount = 2 Then
         ColCount = ColCount + 1
         PCol(ColCount) = i
      Else
         putnumberpresent(1, i) = "*"
      End If
      Next i
   :
   :
```

STEP 19

The second step is to scan the putnumberpresent array to get them in an array of rows, count the number of unique rows and the nodes.

```
   :
   '* collecting all the row numbers in putnumberpresent
   nodecount = 0
   RowCount = 0
   For i = 1 To 9
      PRow(i) = ""
   Next i
   For i = 1 To 9
```

<table>
<tr><td>STEP 19 continued</td><td>

```
        For j = 1 To 9
            If putnumberpresent(1, j) <> "*" And sbox(i, j) = "" And putnumberpresent(i, j)
<> "" Then
                nodecount = nodecount + 1

                PRowFound = 0
                For k = 1 To 9
                  If PRow(k) <> "" Then
                    If PRow(k) = Left(putnumberpresent(i, j), 1) Then
                        PRowFound = 1
                        Exit For
                    End If
                  End If
                Next k
                If PRowFound = 0 Then
                    RowCount = RowCount + 1
                    PRow(RowCount) = Left(putnumberpresent(i, j), 1)
                End If

                PRowFound = 0
                For k = 1 To 9
                  If PRow(k) <> "" Then
                    If PRow(k) = Right(putnumberpresent(i, j), 1) Then
                        PRowFound = 1
                        Exit For
                    End If
                  End If
                Next k
                If PRowFound = 0 Then
                    RowCount = RowCount + 1
                    PRow(RowCount) = Right(putnumberpresent(i, j), 1)
                End If
            End If
        Next j
    Next i
    :
```

</td></tr>
</table>

<table>
<tr><td>STEP 20</td><td>

The third and final step is to first determine if this is a polyomino by comparing the rowcount with the nodecount as discussed earlier, and then if so, adding the putnumber to the cantbelist of the appropriate cells.

```
    :
    :

    If nodecount = 2 * RowCount Then
    ' this check proves that this is a polyomino
      For i = 1 To 9
        For j = 1 To 9
          PRowFound = 0
          PColFound = 0
          For k = 1 To 9
```

</td></tr>
</table>

STEP 20 continued	If PRow(k) <> "" Then
	If PRow(k) + 0 = i Then
	PRowFound = 1
	Exit For
	End If
	End If
	Next k
	For k = 1 To 9
	If PCol(k) <> "" Then
	If PCol(k) + 0 = j Then
	PColFound = 1
	Exit For
	End If
	End If
	Next k
	If PRowFound = 1 And PColFound = 0 And sbox(i, j) = "" Then
	Call addtocantbelist(putnumber, i, j)
	End If
	Next j
	Next i
	End If
	:
	:
	Next putnumber

3.8   MATCHING TWINS

The second algorithm is the matching twins. This is similar to the "love-locked pair" algorithm we discussed earlier, but with a slight difference. The "love-locked pair" was a pair of cells in the same row, column, or 9 by 9 grid with the same two possible numbers. The "love-locked pair" helped us eliminate the numbers from other cells. The "Matching Twin" is the cell itself which has the two possibilities. The point of this algorithm is to *discover* the value of an empty cell, not "*eliminate*" it.

Examine the 9 by 9 matrix and find only those that have exactly two possibilities. For each of these two-possibility cells, fix one of the two numbers and use the rest of the logic you have built so far to get as many blank cells as you can. Now do the same with the other "twin" of the original two-possibility cell. If any of the newly discovered blank cells come up with the same value for both the twins, then this number is a keeper for this blank cell. I will demonstrate this with an example.

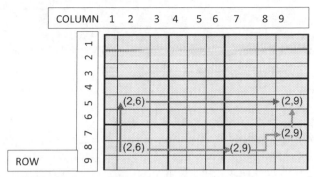

FIGURE 3.9 Matching twins.

In the picture above, the "twins" are identified with the two possible values they can have. Starting from the cell in row 8 column 2, there are two possibilities, 2 and 6. If you assume it is 6 and follow the red arrow, then the cell in row 5 column 9 is 9. If you assume it is 2, and follow the blue arrow, then the cell in row 5 column 9 is 9 as well. Thus "9" is a keeper for the cell in row 5 column 9.

This algorithm also introduces you to the concept of "recursion". I will explain that shortly. But here are the steps to make this algorithm work:

The first step is to take a snapshot of the current 9 by 9 grid so we can compare it later on.

The second step is to make a list of all the cells that have two values since we will have to iterate through this list trying one value each time.

The third step is to pick one of the two-value cells and fill it with one of the two values, run through the rest of the logic and note all the empty cells that got filled—let's call these cells Set 1. Now do the same with the second value and note the empty cells that got filled. Let's call these cells Set 2. Then compare Set 1 with Set 2. If any cell in Set 1 has the same value as Set 2, then this is a keeper. Make a list of these keepers. Let's call these cells Set 3.

The fourth and final step is to restore the snapshot we took in step 1 and then replace the cells in Set 3 with the keepers. We are done!

Here is the code that implements this algorithm.

STEP 21	***First 2 steps to take snapshot and make list of two-value cells.***
| | ```
:
' algorithm to perform matching twins
' * Step 1 take snapshot
For i = 1 To 9
    For j = 1 To 9
        snapshot(i, j) = Cells(i, j)
        putnumberpresent(i, j) = ""
``` |
```

| **STEP 21 continued** | ```
    Next j
Next i
snapshotc = cantbelist
' * Step 2 make a list of all the cells that have 2 values
' * note: this bit of code is from the love-locked pair algorithm
For i = 1 To 9

  For j = 1 To 9
    cantbelistcount(i, j) = 0
    For k = 1 To 9
      If cantbelist(i, j, k) <> 0 Then
        cantbelistcount(i, j) = cantbelistcount(i, j) + 1
      End If
    Next k
    If sbox(i, j) = "" And cantbelistcount(i, j) = 7 Then
      putnumberpresent(i, j) = ""
      For putnumber = 1 To 9
        If findincantbelist(putnumber, i, j) = 0 Then
          putnumberpresent(i, j) = putnumberpresent(i, j) & putnumber
        End If
      Next putnumber
    End If
  Next j
Next i
``` |
| **STEP 22** | ***Next two steps to use each two-value cell and try out one of the values to see if Set 1 = Set 2.***<br>:<br>```
' * Step 3 & 4 Try the 2 values, find values for empty cells for each, check for keepers
(Set 1 = Set 2) and update grid

For i = 1 To 9
  For j = 1 To 9
    If putnumberpresent(i, j) <> "" Then
      ' build S1
        Cells(i, j) = Left(putnumberpresent(i, j), 1)
        sbox(i, j) = Cells(i, j)
        Call RefreshCantbelist
        Call fillemptycells
        For k = 1 To 9
        For l = 1 To 9
          s1(k, l) = Cells(k, l)
        Next l
      Next k
        ' restore snapshot
        For k = 1 To 9
          For l = 1 To 9
            Cells(k, l) = snapshot(k, l)
            sbox(k, l) = snapshot(k, l)
          Next l
``` |

```
                Next k
                cantbelist = snapshotc
                ' build S2
Cells(i, j) = Right(putnumberpresent(i, j), 1)
                sbox(i, j) = Cells(i, j)
                Call fillemptycells
                For k = 1 To 9
                  For l = 1 To 9
                     s2(k, l) = Cells(k, l)
                  Next l
                Next k
                ' restore snapshot
                For k = 1 To 9
                  For l = 1 To 9
                     Cells(k, l) = snapshot(k, l)
                     sbox(k, l) = snapshot(k, l)
                  Next l
                Next k
                cantbelist = snapshotc
                'compare s1 and s2


For k = 1 To 9
  For l = 1 To 9
        If s1(k, l) <> snapshot(k, l) And s2(k, l) = s1(k, l) Then
           Cells(k, l) = s1(k, l)
           sbox(k, l) = s1(k, l)
           snapshot(k, l) = s1(k, l)
        End If
     Next l
   Next k
   Call RefreshCantbelist
 End If
 Next j
Next i
```

We also need these functions that are called in the code.

```
Sub fillemptycells()
'first check all cells - if 8 numbers in cantbelist, then we know the number

  For i = 1 To 9
    For j = 1 To 9
    If sbox(i, j) = "" Then
      whatisthisnumber = 0
      For k = 1 To 9
      If cantbelist(i, j, k) > 0 Then
        howmanycantbe = k
        whatisthisnumber = whatisthisnumber + cantbelist(i, j, k)
      End If
    Next k
    If howmanycantbe = 8 Then
```

```
            sbox(i, j) = 45 - whatisthisnumber
            Cells(i, j) = sbox(i, j)
            Call updatecantbelist(sbox(i, j), i, j)
         End If
      End If
      Next j
      Next i


' now check all columns row by row for all numbers 1-9 (putnumber)
' if the number is invalid in 8 of the nine cells in the same row, then the number
' must belong to the ninth cell (empty, of course)


For putnumber = 1 To 9
:
   For i = 1 To 9
      numberfound = 0

   For j = 1 To 9
      If sbox(i, j) = putnumber Then numberfound = 1
   Next j

         If numberfound = 0 Then
            notahomecount = 0
            For j = 1 To 9
               notahome = 0
               If sbox(i, j) <> "" Then notahome = 1
               For k = 1 To 9
                  If cantbelist(i, j, k) = putnumber Then notahome = 1
               Next k
               If notahome = 1 Then
                  notahomecount = notahomecount + 1
               Else
                  home = j
               End If
            Next j
            If notahomecount = 8 Then
               sbox(i, home) = putnumber
               Call updatecantbelist(putnumber, i, home)
               Cells(i, home) = sbox(i, home)
            End If
         End If
      Next i

' now check all rows column by column for all numbers 1-9 (putnumber)
' if the number is invalid in 8 of the nine cells in the same column, then the number
' must belong to the ninth cell (empty, of course)


   For j = 1 To 9
      numberfound = 0
```

STEP 22 Continued (fill emptycells)

```
For i = 1 To 9
   If sbox(i, j) = putnumber Then numberfound = 1
Next i


      If numberfound = 0 Then
         notahomecount = 0
         For i = 1 To 9
            notahome = 0
            If sbox(i, j) <> "" Then notahome = 1
            For k = 1 To 9
               If cantbelist(i, j, k) = putnumber Then notahome = 1
            Next k
            If notahome = 1 Then
               notahomecount = notahomecount + 1
            Else
               home = i
            End If
         Next i
         If notahomecount = 8 Then
            sbox(home, j) = putnumber
            Call updatecantbelist(putnumber, home, j)
            Cells(home, j) = sbox(home, j)
         End If
      End If
   Next j

' now check all cells in the 3x3 boxes for all numbers 1-9 (putnumber)
' if the number is invalid in 8 of the nine cells in the same 3x3 box, then the number
' must belong to the ninth cell (empty, of course)

For i = 1 To 3
   For j = 1 To 3
      For k = 1 To 3
         n = Int((i - 1) / 3) * 3 + k
         For l = 1 To 3
            p = Int((j - 1) / 3) * 3 + l
            numberfound = 0
            If sbox(n, p) = putnumber Then numberfound = 1
         Next l
      Next k

   If numberfound = 0 Then
      notahomecount = 0
      For k = 1 To 3
         n = Int((i - 1) / 3) * 3 + k
         For l = 1 To 3
            p = Int((j - 1) / 3) * 3 + l
            notahome = 0
```

| STEP 22 Continued (fill emptycells) | ```
          If sbox(n, p) <> "" Then notahome = 1
          For kk = 1 To 9
             If cantbelist(n, p, kk) = putnumber Then notahome = 1
          Next kk
          If notahome = 1 Then
             notahomecount = notahomecount + 1
          Else
             homerow = n
             homecol = p
          End If
        Next l
      Next k
      If notahomecount = 8 Then
          sbox(homerow, homecol) = putnumber
          Call updatecantbelist(putnumber, homerow, homecol)
          Cells(homerow, homecol) = sbox(homerow, homecol)
        End If
      End If
   Next j
   Next i
   :

Next putnumber
End Sub
``` |
| STEP 22 Continued (Refreshcantbelist) | ```
Sub RefreshCantbelist()
   For i = 1 To 9
     For j = 1 To 9
      For k = 1 To 9
   '*        check all columns in this row
        If j <> k Then
          ' For m = 1 To 9
          If sbox(i, k) > 0 Then
             foundincantbelist = 0
             For kk = 1 To 9
             If sbox(i, k) = cantbelist(i, j, kk) Then foundincantbelist = 1
             Next kk
             If foundincantbelist = 0 Then
             cantbelist(i, j, NextEmptyLocation(i, j)) = sbox(i, k)
             End If
          End If
          'Next m
        End If
      Next k
   '*        check all rows in this column
      For k = 1 To 9
        If i <> k Then
           ' For m = 1 To 9
           If sbox(k, j) > 0 Then
             foundincantbelist = 0
             For kk = 1 To 9
``` |

STEP 22 Continued (Refreshcantbelist)

```
                If sbox(k, j) = cantbelist(i, j, kk) Then foundincantbelist = 1
                Next kk
                If foundincantbelist - 0 Then
                cantbelist(i, j, NextEmptyLocation(i, j)) = sbox(k, j)
              End If
            End If
          ' Next m
        End If
      Next k
      '*          check all cells in the 3x3 box this cell belongs to

      For k = 1 To 3
        n = Int((i - 1) / 3) * 3 + k
        For l = 1 To 3
          p = Int((j - 1) / 3) * 3 + l
          If (i = n And j = p) Then
            m = m 'do nothing
          Else

          If sbox(n, p) <> "" Then
            foundincantbelist = 0
            For kk = 1 To 9
            If sbox(n, p) = cantbelist(i, j, kk) Then foundincantbelist = 1
            Next kk
            If foundincantbelist = 0 Then
            cantbelist(i, j, NextEmptyLocation(i, j)) = sbox(n, p)
            End If
          End If

          End If
        Next l
      Next k


      Next j
    Next i
  End Sub
```

3.9 CONCLUSION

Playing a Sudoku game is very entertaining. But to be able to solve it using your own program is priceless. This chapter helps you to see the numerous patterns, which, once coded into an algorithm, yield a surprising answer through the power of iteration. This macro makes solving Sudoku much faster than a human being can!

There is a rather simple strategy that one can apply to Sudoku games—fill in the blanks with the nine possible digits (1–9) and check if all the rows, columns, and 3 by 3 squares have unrepeated digits. But this algorithm takes very long to yield a result.

This is because typically a Sudoku has 70 blank squares, hence, there can be 9^{70} combinations that you will need to test. This is a staggering sum of 6,265,787,482,177,97 0,000,000,000,000,000,000,000,000,000,000,000,000,000,000,000,000! This is likely to take a long time for the processor to calculate.

In this chapter you also learned the following coding terms:

- Arrays
- How to navigate a matrix
- How to call other programs (subroutines or "Subs" from one program)
- Nested If Statements
- Nested For statements

I want to leave you with a problem—what if you want to generate a game instead of solving it? How would you develop the algorithm for it? Remember that any arrangement of 81 squares, some of which are unfilled, do not qualify to be a game. You must be sure that it can be solved and that there is one and only one solution.

4 Introduction to Multiplatform Integration
Build Your Own Remote Control

A lever is a simple machine that reduces the effort required to lift a heavy load. I find levers fascinating because these were one of the first machines invented by humans and have laid the foundation for all present-day machines that rely on a mechanical principle. The discovery of the lever is largely credited to Archimedes in the third century BC, who made this sentence famous "Give me a place to stand, and I will move the world".

Fast forward to the 21st century, human inventions have reached new heights. Artificial intelligence is a reality. Electric cars are commercially available, and driverless versions of these cars will be commonplace on our roads soon. With a smartphone in our hand, a laptop on our desk, and Alexa playing our favorite tune, we "facetime" our friends and family whenever we want. We have powerful tools readily available in our hands! We have come a long way from the simple lever. Yet, there is so much more to innovate—so much more power to be harnessed in order to utilize these marvelous machines to their full potential.

During a meeting I recently attended, a speaker was presenting material through slides, from the podium, facing the audience. The slides were presented on a big screen for the audience to view. However, the slide show was being controlled by another team member designated to manage the presentation for all speakers, further away in the audio control booth. This unavoidable situation is a result of shared equipment and common slide decks. The speaker had to wait for the team member to advance the slide. This delay caused awkward silences throughout the presentation.

It made me think about how to make this process more efficient. The team member and the speaker had two different roles—one to coordinate the presentation files and another to present the material that was pertinent for the speaker's specific topic. How could we design a technical solution that covered both requirements in a seamless way?

Could we solve this problem with a program that can be operated from the speaker's smartphone to move the slides?

While there are existing apps to control a presentation from a smartphone, it is easy to build your own program to achieve the same results and more! To make this magic happen you require one more piece of software—googledocs. It has the unique

DOI: 10.1201/9781003214335-5

capability of operating both on a computer and a smartphone. The added benefit of this program is that in addition to moving the slides, the speaker can present content "on the fly", directly from the smartphone. For example, the speaker can now add impromptu short messages or thank you notes as required over the existing slides! The remote control is now in the hands of the speaker!

This chapter describes the workings of this simple program.

The system has two basic parts:

- A powerpoint slide pack that needs to be moved from slide to slide on your laptop/desktop.
- A remote control device which is a small file on googledocs manipulated through the googledocs app on your smartphone.

4.1 CONNECTING THE SMARTPHONE TO THE LAPTOP – VIRTUALLY

Both laptop and smartphone need to be connected to the internet for the magic to work.

The program enables the powerpoint slides on the laptop/desktop to read the googledocs file maintained from the smartphone and moves the slides based on its contents. In order to make it meaningful, we need to come up with a set of codes that can be interpreted by the program to do useful actions.

Once the connection between these two components is established, you can set up any code you like—there is no limit to creativity! But this is a set that does some basic jobs and a bit more.

B	Blank out this slide
N	Go to Next Slide
P	Go to Previous Slide
#	Start or end of text to display
X	Exit from the program

Googledocs puts you document in the cloud and allows you to access it using a URL. This is the property that we can exploit to write this novel program. The following link points to the file that has been created to drive the program.

https://docs.google.com/document/d/1-6ZjkbA9nM1gCCIkot0dimp5Wmu5ZIPg B1DjoPB5eDo/edit?usp=sharing

This document has its sharing parameter set so that anyone can update it. You can, of course set your own parameters with your own document. A document is just a blank file with a marker-text (explained in the next paragraph). Just remember to change the link in the program.

It is important for the program to know where to read from in the file. For this reason, we have created a marker-text—"SlideMover". When the program reads this text, it knows to start reading from the very next character.

The code for the powerpoint sits in a macro. But then you would not know which slide deck you need to work with in advance. So the macro is in its own powerpoint deck with only one slide in it. This slide has a picture that kicks off the macro by clicking on it. See example below on how to set up this slide. To start off we need a picture—in this example this is a man playing the trumpet.

4.2   SETTINGS IN POWERPOINT

If you select the picture and click your right mouse, you get a menu somewhat like this.

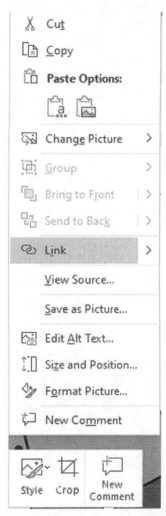

FIGURE 4.1   Picture menu.

If you now click on the "Link" option, you get a screen where you can choose the name of the macro you would like to execute—in this case it is called SlideMover.

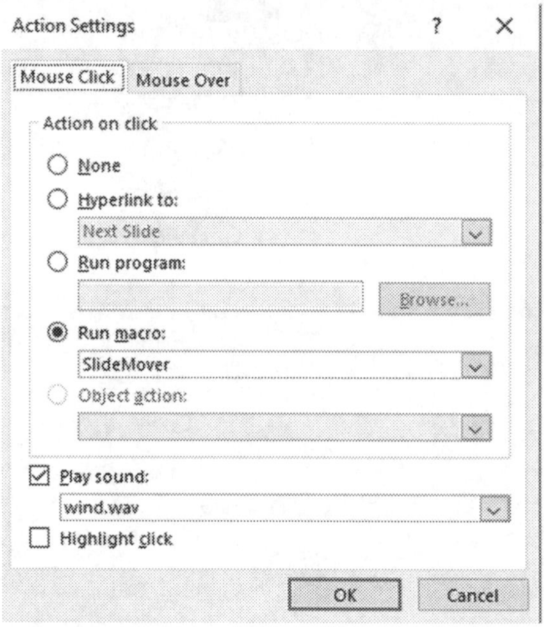

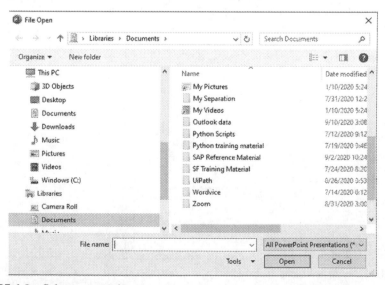

FIGURE 4.2   Action setting.

You are able to execute the code by running this one slide powerpoint deck in presentation mode and then clicking on the picture.

Step 1 is to recognize and initiate the presentation that you want to control. It brings up a file dialog box like below and allows you to choose the powerpoint file of your choice.

FIGURE 4.3   Select presentation.

4.3   STANDARD FUNCTIONS

A standard function can be used to locate and open the presentation. The standard function belongs to a class of similar functions commonly referred to as "Application". The function itself (Application.FileDialog) returns an object of type FileDialog, which stores the name and path chosen and can be queried later on to use in operations.

Another standard function (Presentations.Open) is used to open the powerpoint presentation file and while opening can be set to a slide show mode by a parameter called ShowType.

Here is the code that does this:

```
Sub SlideMover()

Dim ie As Object
Dim form As Variant
Dim pptSlide As Slide
Dim pptLayout As CustomLayout
Dim button As Variant
Dim LR As Integer
Dim var As String
Dim var1 As Object
Dim oHEle As HTMLULIstElement ' Create HTML element (<ul>) object.
Dim sldOne As Slide
Dim MyCallout As Shape
Dim dlgOpen As FileDialog
ActivePresentation.SlideShowWindow.View.Exit

Set dlgOpen = Application.FileDialog(Type:=msoFileDialogOpen)

    With dlgOpen
       .AllowMultiSelect = False
       .Show
    End With
filepath = dlgOpen.SelectedItems.Item(1)
Set objPresentation = Presentations.Open(filepath, True)
objPresentation.Windows(1).Activate
With objPresentation.SlideShowSettings
    .ShowType = ppShowSpeaker
    .Run.View.AcceleratorsEnabled = False
End With
SlideNumber = 1
PreviousLen = 1
Call HeavyLifting
End Sub
```

STEP 1

4.4   READING THE GOOGLEDOCS INPUT

Next, we need to read the input from the googledocs document. This is done by the subroutine called "HeavyLifting" in the code in step 1.

STEP 2—Initialization	*This code is required to set up the variables used in this program.*
	
	Sub HeavyLifting()
	
	Dim ie As Object
	Dim form As Variant
	Dim pptSlide As Slide
	Dim pptLayout As CustomLayout
	Dim button As Variant
	Dim LR As Integer
	Dim var As String
	Dim var1 As Object
	Dim oHEle As HTMLULListElement ' Create HTML element (<ul>) object.
	Dim sldOne As Slide
	Dim MyCallout As Shape
	Dim dlgOpen As FileDialog
	' *** this is the link to the googledocs that controls the slides
	' https://docs.google.com/document/d/1-6ZjkbA9nM1gCCIkot0dimp5Wmu5ZIPgB1D
	joPB5eDo/edit?usp=sharing
	' *** must have the word "SlideMover" to begin. N means forward. P means backward.
	' *** a # is the beginning of text to display, expects another # before it displays
	' *** text is recognized as a web link and will display in full screen if it contains the word http (will show in white)
	' *** B will blank out a screen. Another B will bring it back
	' *** X stops the control from the macro
	' *** Manual navigation possible with up. down arrow, left right arrow, or P and N.
	   thisTime = currentTime
	   PreviousVar = ""
	   TotalSlides = objPresentation.Slides.Count
	   ShowText = ""
	   FirstT = 0
	   WhiteScreen = 0
	   LaunchLink = 0
	   'objPresentation.Windows(1).Activate

STEP 2—read googledocs	*The googledocs document is read every second until the end of the slide pack is reached. It has only one record, hence the loop "Do Until EOF" is commented out. The length of the record is checked. If the length is greater than it was previously, then this indicated that the user has entered an input. This additional input is stored in the variable "CommandWord" for further action.*
	
	   While (ActivePresentation.SlideShowWindow.View.CurrentShowPosition <= TotalSlides) And ForcedExit = 0
	     ManualInterrupt
	     Sleep (1000)
	     myURL = https://docs.google.com/document/d/1-6ZjkbA9nM1gCCIkot0dimp5Wmu5ZIPgB1DjoPB5eDo/edit?usp=sharing

| **STEP 2—read googledocs** | ```
    Set HttpReq = CreateObject("Microsoft.XMLHTTP")
      HttpReq.Open "GET", myURL, False, "", ""
      HttpReq.send
      myURL = HttpReq.responseBody
      If HttpReq.Status = 200 Then
         Set oStrm = CreateObject("ADODB.Stream")
         oStrm.Open
         oStrm.Type = 1
         oStrm.Write HttpReq.responseBody
         oStrm.SaveToFile filepath, 2 ' 1 = no overwrite, 2 = overwrite
         oStrm.Close
      End If
      Open filepath For Input As #1
      'Do Until EOF(1)
         Line Input #1, LineFromFile
         StartPosition = InStr(LineFromFile, "SlideMover") + 9
         EndPosition = InStr(StartPosition, LineFromFile, """")
         c = EndPosition - StartPosition
         If c > PreviousLen Then
            CommandWord = Mid(LineFromFile, StartPosition + PreviousLen, c
- PreviousLen)
            PreviousLen = c
         Else
           If c < PreviousLen Then
             PreviousLen = c
             CommandWord = ""
           Else
             CommandWord = ""
           End If
         End If
      'Loop
      Close #1
``` |
| **STEP 2—read input and take action** | ```
      If CommandWord = "" Then
         Else
            If LaunchLink = 2 Then
               Call ReturnToPresentation
               Exit Sub
               LaunchLink = 0
            End If
            If FirstT = 0 Then
               If InStr(CommandWord, "B") > 0 Then
               If WhiteScreen = 0 Then
                  Set pptLayout = ActivePresentation.Slides(1).CustomLayout
                  Set pptSlide = ActivePresentation.Slides.
AddSlide(ActivePresentation.SlideShowWindow.View.CurrentShowPosition,
pptLayout)
                  PreviousSlide
                  WhiteScreen = 1

            Else
``` |

STEP 2—read input and take action (continued)

```
ActivePresentation.Slides(ActivePresentation.SlideShowWindow.View.
CurrentShowPosition).Delete
            NextSlide
            WhiteScreen = 0

          End If
        Else
          If InStr(CommandWord, "N") > 0 Then
            NextSlide
            SlideNumber = SlideNumber + 1
          Else
            If InStr(CommandWord, "P") > 0 Then
              PreviousSlide
              SlideNumber = SlideNumber - 1
            Else
              d = InStr(CommandWord, "#")
              If d > 0 Then
                e = InStr(d + 1, CommandWord, "#")
                If e > 0 Then
                  ShowText = Mid(CommandWord, d + 1, e - d - 1)
                  SlideNumber = ActivePresentation.SlideShowWindow.View.
CurrentShowPosition
                  Call AddCallout(ShowText, SlideNumber)
                  ShowText = ""
                  FirstT = 0

                Else
                FirstT = 1
                ShowText = Mid(CommandWord, d + 1, 100)
                SlideNumber = ActivePresentation.SlideShowWindow.View.
CurrentShowPosition
                  Call AddCallout(ShowText, SlideNumber)
                End If
    :
    :
    :

                Else
              End If
            End If
          End If
        End If
      Else
        d = InStr(CommandWord, "#")
        If d > 0 Then
          ShowText = ShowText & Mid(CommandWord, 1, d - 1)
          SlideNumber = ActivePresentation.SlideShowWindow.View.
CurrentShowPosition
          Call AddCallout(ShowText, SlideNumber)
          If LaunchLink = 1 Then
```

<table>
<tr><td rowspan="1">STEP 2—read input and take action (continued)</td><td>

```
            LaunchLink = 2
            Call AddMedia(ShowText)
         End If
         ShowText = ""
         FirstT = 0
         'Sleep (1000)
      Else
         ShowText = ShowText & CommandWord
         SlideNumber = ActivePresentation.SlideShowWindow.View.
CurrentShowPosition
         Call AddCallout(ShowText, SlideNumber)
       End If
     End If
     If CommandWord = "X" Then
       MsgBox ("Bye")
       Exit Sub
     End If


   End If



   Wend
  ActivePresentation.Close
End Sub
```

</td></tr>
</table>

In step 2 when a "#" is entered, the program goes into "receiving" mode and collects the characters that are entered. These are not displayed until another "#" is entered, signifying the end of the text. Then this text is displayed in the current slide in a bubble. The different states of the text input are controlled through a variable called "LaunchLink" in the code above.

The code in step 2 also calls a few other functions. These are provided in Section 4.1.

<table>
<tr><td rowspan="1">STEP 2 Functions</td><td>

```
Sub NextSlide()
     ActivePresentation.SlideShowWindow.View.Next
End Sub
Sub PreviousSlide()
     ActivePresentation.SlideShowWindow.View.Previous
End Sub
Sub OnSlideShowPageChange()
     Dim i As Integer
     i = ActivePresentation.SlideShowWindow.View.CurrentShowPosition
End Sub
Sub AddCallout(ShowText, SlideNumber)
     Dim MyCallout As Shape
     Set sldOne = ActivePresentation.Slides(ActivePresentation.SlideShowWindow.
View.CurrentShowPosition)
     On Error GoTo CallOutCreate:
     sldOne.Shapes("Impromptu").TextFrame.TextRange.Text = ShowText
```

</td></tr>
</table>

STEP 2 Functions (continued)

```
        If InStr(ShowText, "http") > 0 Then
            MyCallout.Fill.ForeColor.RGB = RGB(255, 255, 255)
            LaunchLink = 1
        End If
        Application.SlideShowWindows(1).View.GotoSlide (ActivePresentation.
SlideShowWindow.View.CurrentShowPosition)
Exit Sub
CallOutCreate:
        Set MyCallout = sldOne.Shapes.AddCallout(Type:=msoCalloutTwo, Left:=50,
Top:=50, _
        Width:=200, Height:=100)
        MyCallout.TextFrame.AutoSize = ppAutoSizeShapeToFitText
        MyCallout.TextFrame.TextRange.Text = ShowText
        MyCallout.Name = "Impromptu"
        If InStr(ShowText, "http") > 0 Then
            MyCallout.Fill.ForeColor.RGB = RGB(255, 255, 255)
            LaunchLink = 1
        End If
        Application.SlideShowWindows(1).View.GotoSlide (ActivePresentation.
SlideShowWindow.View.CurrentShowPosition)
End Sub
Sub AddMedia(ShowText)
    Dim osld As Slide
    Dim ovid As Shape
    Dim sldOne As Slide
    Set sldOne = ActivePresentation.Slides(ActivePresentation.SlideShowWindow.View.
CurrentShowPosition)
    PresentationName = sldOne.Name

    SlideNumber = ActivePresentation.SlideShowWindow.View.CurrentShowPosition
    Set Web = CreateObject("InternetExplorer.Application")
    Web.Visible = True
    Web.FullScreen = True
    Web.navigate ShowText
    End Sub
    Sub ReturnToPresentation()
    'Set objPresentation = Presentations(PresentationName)
objPresentation.Windows(1).Activate
    ActivePresentation.SlideShowWindow.View.Exit
objPresentation.SlideShowSettings.Run
    Application.SlideShowWindows(1).View.GotoSlide (SlideNumber)
Call HeavyLifting
End Sub
```

4.5   TAKING OVER KEYBOARD CONTROLS

Finally, since the presentation is initiated through a program, it may not respond
to the usual keyboard controls. This needs to be taken care of through a predefined

function called GetAsyncKeyState that is available for use but has to be declared upfront (see step 1 code). The code below covers some of the basic navigations that can be done by the user near the laptop, without using the smartphone. The letter "N", Right or Down keys take you to next slide. The letter "P", Up, or Left keys take you to the previous slide. The "X" key is to exit the program.

STEP 3

```
Sub ManualInterrupt()
Const VK_CONTROL = &H11, VK_LEFT = &H25, VK_UP = &H26, VK_
RIGHT = &H27, VK_DOWN = &H28
Const VK_0 = &H30, VK_1 = &H31, VK_2 = &H32, VK_3 = &H33, VK_4 = &H34
Const VK_5 = &H35, VK_6 = &H36, VK_7 = &H37, VK_8 = &H38, VK_9 = &H39
Const VK_A = &H41, VK_B = &H42, VK_C = &H43, VK_D = &H44, VK_
E = &H45
Const VK_F = &H46, VK_G = &H47, VK_H = &H48, VK_I = &H49, VK_J = &H4A
Const VK_K = &H4B, VK_L = &H4C, VK_M = &H4D, VK_N = &H4E, VK_
O = &H4F
Const VK_P = &H50, VK_Q = &H51, VK_R = &H52, VK_S = &H53, VK_T = &H54
Const VK_U = &H55, VK_V = &H56, VK_W = &H57, VK_X = &H58, VK_
Y = &H59, VK_Z = &H5A
Const VK_ENTER = &HD

    If GetAsyncKeyState(VK_X) <> 0 Then
        ' MsgBox ("forced exit")
        ForcedExit = 1
        MsgBox ("Forced")
    End If
    If GetAsyncKeyState(VK_DOWN) <> 0 Then
        NextSlide
    End If
    If GetAsyncKeyState(VK_RIGHT) <> 0 Then
        NextSlide
    End If
    If GetAsyncKeyState(VK_UP) <> 0 Then
        PreviousSlide
    End If
    If GetAsyncKeyState(VK_LEFT) <> 0 Then
        PreviousSlide
    End If
    If GetAsyncKeyState(VK_P) <> 0 Then
        PreviousSlide
    End If
    If GetAsyncKeyState(VK_N) <> 0 Then
        NextSlide
    End If
End Sub
```

Note—VBA code in powerpoint is slightly different than in excel—some commands and functions used in excel do not work in powerpoint.

While there are commercial tools available to control presentations remotely, this program has two unique features that are not readily available:

- It allows more than one person to control the presentation, making it a collaborative tool—thanks to the versatile nature of googledocs.
- It allows a remote person to show text on a slide that is being presented—while this may sound scary, it is very useful at times when a coauthor of a slide deck wants to emphasize a point or bring in a humorous or impactful comment to the audience. Imagine during a sales presentation you realize that you forgot to provide the contact number of the salesperson in the deck—you can enter it in your googledocs and it will be shown in the current slide without interrupting the flow of the deck!

4.6   CONCLUSION

This chapter is an experiment in automation. It is an introduction for you to explore the possibilities of connecting one system with another and creating magic! The hope is that this program will give you the inspiration to explore integration opportunities according to your needs.

In this chapter you also learned:

- Working with powerpoint and VBA
- Presentation objects
- Simulating key strokes
- https (web) objects

Here are two extensions of this problem that you might find interesting to work on your own—how can you make little red dots appear on the current slide remotely? And how can you completely close the presentation?

5 The Organizer
Build Your Own Virtual Filing Cabinet

Organizing is a core skill. When computers were not so prevalent and most businesses relied on paper documents, it became important to organize the paperwork so that one can retrieve it when needed. A filing system remains the central record-keeping system for any organization. However, we do not find large filing cabinets anymore because files have become electronic. But the ability to find the records when needed is still as important.

Modern office productivity systems have made it quite easy to store a file in the "right" place soon after one creates the file. But once created, it is not always easy to find it. The mnemonic principle of associative memory is pulled into use and is dependent on the answer to the question—where is the logical place one would keep such a document? For example, if it is an invoice, one would look under "Customer Invoices" in the folder structure, and then search it alphabetically to find the right file name. There is some amount of faith involved in this exercise—that the person who created it remembered to name the file with the customer's name in front and remembered to put it in the "Customer Invoices" folder. If the file was not named in the expected format, it might be hard to retrieve it.

One way to resolve this issue is to have a list of all files. And, if we have this list in a spreadsheet, it will be easy to search for the file.

This chapter describes how this can be done quite simply, with a macro. One additional skill you can pick up is how to create a progress message when this program takes longer than expected. This is important since the human mind gets tired of waiting if it does not know how long one has to wait (the proverbial "are we there yet" syndrome!).

The algorithm works in six steps:

5.1 THE ALGORITHM

Step 1: Set up a worksheet with the appropriate headings and tab names to display the files

Step 2: Get the user to select the starting point from which the search must begin

Step 3: Get a count for all files and folders in the chosen path and prepare status bar

Step 4: Monitor time elapsed and give user a chance to exit if it is taking too long

DOI: 10.1201/9781003214335-6

Step 5: Get all file and folder names and store in the new worksheet(s) created in step 1

Step 6: Save in a new workbook

Note that steps 3 and 5 are similar, because you have to read the headers of all file objects to determine how many there are. It is necessary to do this so that a message with progress status can be displayed.

Note that the code in steps 3 and 5 calls itself. This is known as "recursion".

Here is the code:

<table>
<tr><td rowspan="1">STEP 1</td><td>

```
Public i As Double, k As Double, wb As Workbook, ws As Worksheet, j As Double,
NoData As Integer, B As String
Public OverallTime As Double
Public fs As New FileSystemObject
Public FSO As New FileSystemObject
Sub Macro1()
Dim A As String, Folder As String, FileName As String

  B = Now
  OverallTime = 0
  'A = DateDiff("s", Now, B)



  Set wb = Workbooks.Add
    With wb
      .Worksheets(1).Name = "Folders"
    End With

  Set ws = wb.Sheets.Add
    With ws
      .Name = "Errors"
    End With

  wb.Sheets("Folders").Activate

  NoData = 0
  i = 2
  k = 1
  Cells(1, 1) = "Name"
  Cells(1, 2) = "Type"
  Cells(1, 3) = "Size"
  Cells(1, 4) = "Path"
  Cells(1, 5) = "Last Modified on"
  Call PickFolder(Folder)
  j = 0
  Set FSO = CreateObject("Scripting.FileSystemObject")
  Call GetFolderNames2(Folder)
```

</td></tr>
</table>

STEP 1 continued	Call GetFolderNames(Folder)
	
	If NoData = 0 Then
	   Call PickFile(FileName)
	End If
	Application.StatusBar = False
	End Sub

STEP 2	Sub PickFolder(Folder)
	   Dim fldr As FileDialog
	   Dim sItem As String
	   Set fldr = Application.FileDialog(msoFileDialogFolderPicker)
	   With fldr
	     .Title = "Please Select a Folder by clicking (mandatory)"
	     .AllowMultiSelect = False
	     .InitialFileName = Application.DefaultFilePath
	     If .Show <> -1 Then GoTo NextCode
	     sItem = .SelectedItems(1)
	   End With
	NextCode:
	   If (InStr(1, sItem, "\") < Len(sItem)) Then
	     Folder = sItem & "\"
	   Else
	     Folder = sItem
	   End If
	   Set fldr = Nothing
	End Sub

STEP 3	Sub GetFolderNames2(Folder)
	   Dim SubFolders As Variant
	   Dim FileItem As Object
	   Dim SourceFolder As Object
	   Dim FolderNames() As String
	   Call TimeLimit
	   FolderNameIndex = 0
	   Set SourceFolder = FSO.GetFolder(Folder)
	   If j = 0 Then
	     For Each FileItem In SourceFolder.Files
	       On Error GoTo errorresume
	       A = FileItem.Name
	       j = j + 1
	       Application.StatusBar = " Preparing the computation: Number of rows " & j &
	" Time is " & Now
	     Next
	   End If
	   On Error GoTo errorresume
	   A = Dir$(Folder, vbDirectory)
	   Do While A <> ""

| **STEP 3 continued** | ```
        If A <> "." And A <> ".." Then
            If FSO.folderExists(Folder & A) Then
            FolderNameIndex = FolderNameIndex + 1
            ReDim Preserve FolderNames(FolderNameIndex)
            FolderNames(FolderNameIndex) = Folder & A & "\"
        End If
        j = j + 1
        Application.StatusBar = " Preparing the computation: Number of rows " & j & "
Time is " & Now
        End If
        A = Dir$()
    Loop
        ' Recursion
    If FolderNameIndex > 0 Then
        For jj = 1 To FolderNameIndex
            Call GetFolderNames2(FolderNames(jj))
        Next
    End If
    Exit Sub
    Application.StatusBar = " Preparing the computation: Number of rows " & j & "
Time is " & Now
errorresume:
    N = j
End Sub
``` |
| **STEP 4** | *Note here the clever use of the MOD function. The MOD function provides a remainder. By checking for the remainder when the overall time is divided by 300, we implement a checkpoint for the user every five minutes.*<br>```
Sub TimeLimit()
Y = DateDiff("s", B, Now)
If Y Mod 300 > 295 Then
    OverallTime = OverallTime + Y / 60
    X = InputBox("Already 5 more minutes passed" & " a total of " &
Round(OverallTime, 2) & " minutes - do u want to continue? ")
    If Left(X, 1) = "Y" Or Left(X, 1) = "y" Then
    Else
        End
    End If
End If
End Sub
``` |
| **STEP 5** | ```
Sub GetFolderNames(Folder)
    Dim FolderNames() As String
    Dim SubFolders As Variant
    Dim FileItem As Object
    Dim SourceFolder As Object
    FolderNameIndex = 0
    Set fs = CreateObject("Scripting.FileSystemObject")
    Set SourceFolder = FSO.GetFolder(Folder)
``` |
```

STEP 5 continued

```
    If i = 2 Then
        For Each FileItem In SourceFolder.Files
            On Error GoTo errorresume
            A = FileItem.Name
            Call PopulateRow(i, A, Folder)
            i = i + 1
            Application.StatusBar = " Number of rows " & (i - 2) & " of " & j & " complete
" & Round((i - 2) / j * 100, 0) & " Percent " & " Expected remaining duration " &
Round(OverallTime * (j - i + 2) * 60 / j, 0) & " seconds"
        Next
    End If
    On Error GoTo errorresume
    A = Dir$(Folder, vbDirectory)
        Do While A <> ""
            If (A <> "." And A <> "..") Then
                Call PopulateRow(i, A, Folder)
                If fs.folderExists(Folder & A) Then
                    FolderNameIndex = FolderNameIndex + 1
                    ReDim Preserve FolderNames(FolderNameIndex)
                    FolderNames(FolderNameIndex) = Folder & A & "\"
                End If
                i = i + 1
                Application.StatusBar = " Number of rows " & (i - 2) & " of " & j & "
complete " & Round((i - 2) / j * 100, 0) & " Percent " & " Expected remaining duration
" & Round(OverallTime * (j - i + 2) * 60 / j, 0) & " seconds"
            End If
            A = Dir$()
        Loop
        If FolderNameIndex > 0 Then
            For jj = 1 To FolderNameIndex
                Call GetFolderNames(FolderNames(jj))
            Next
        End If
        Exit Sub
errorresume:
        wb.Sheets("Errors").Activate
        Cells(k, 1) = "Folder/File inaccessible! " & Folder & "\" & A
        k = k + 1
        wb.Sheets("Folders").Activate
End Sub
    Dim F As Folder
    Dim FI As File
    Application.StatusBar = " Number of rows " & (i - 2) & " of " & j & " complete
" & Round((i - 2) / j * 100, 0) & " Percent " & " Expected remaining duration " &
Round(OverallTime * (j - i + 2) * 60 / j, 0) & " seconds"
    Set fs = CreateObject("Scripting.FileSystemObject")
    If B <> "." And B <> ".." Then
        Cells(i, 1) = B
        'Cells(i, 2) = GetAttr(Folder & B)
```

```
'Cells(i, 2) = GetAttr(Folder)
If Right(Folder & B, 1) <> "\" Then
    FolderPath = Folder & B & "\"
Else
Sub PopulateRow(ByRef i As Double, ByVal B As String, ByVal Folder As String)
    FolderPath = Folder & B
End If
If fs.folderExists(FolderPath) Then
    Set F = fs.GetFolder(FolderPath)
    Cells(i, 2) = "FOLDER"
Else
    Set FI = fs.GetFile(Folder & B)
    Cells(i, 2) = "FILE"
End If
On Error GoTo Errormessage
If Cells(i, 2).Value = "FOLDER" Then
    M = F.Attributes
    'If M And 16 Then
    'M = 1
    'End If
    Cells(i, 3) = F.Size
    Cells(i, 4) = F.Path
Cells(i, 5) = F.DateLastModified
Cells(i, 6) = F.Attributes
Else
    M = FI.Attributes
    N = 0
    If M And 32 Then
    N = 1
    End If
    N = 0
    If M = 0 Then
    N = 99
    End If
    Cells(i, 3) = FI.Size
    Cells(i, 4) = FI.Path
    Cells(i, 5) = FI.DateLastModified
    Cells(i, 6) = FI.Attributes

End If
Exit Sub
Errormessage:
    Cells(i, 3) = "no access"
    Cells(i, 4) = "no access"
    Cells(i, 5) = "no access"
End If
End Sub
```

<table>
<tr><td>STEP 6</td><td>

```
Sub PickFile(FileName)
    Dim fldr As FileDialog
    Dim sItem As String
    Set fldr = Application.FileDialog(msoFileDialogSaveAs)
    With fldr
        .Title = "Save as"
        .InitialFileName = "test.xlsx"
        .FilterIndex = 1
        If .Show <> 0 Then
            FileName = .SelectedItems(1)
            ActiveWorkbook.SaveAs FileName:=.SelectedItems(1)
        End If
    End With
End Sub
```

</td></tr>
</table>

5.2 INVOKING THE CODE

Now that the program is written, you will need a mechanism to invoke it. While there are many ways to do this, a quick and easy way is to add a rectangular shape on the sheet that doubles as a button.

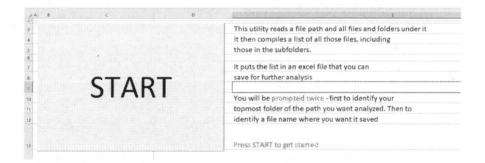

FIGURE 5.1 Invoke macro from rectangle shape.

Below is a sample output.

Name	Type	Size	Path	Last Modified on
ACS - Augmenting Common Sense with Spreadsheets.docx	FILE	1081314	C:\Users\deepa\Documents\My Creativity\ACS - Augmenting Common Sense with Spreadsheets.docx	9/11/2020 12:19
address-information-api.pdf	FILE	494673	C:\Users\deepa\Documents\My Creativity\address-information-api.pdf	4/11/2020 10:24
Algorithm for Web Scraping using VBA.docx	FILE	732357	C:\Users\deepa\Documents\My Creativity\Algorithm for Web Scraping using VBA.docx	4/13/2020 18:24
Algorithm for Web Scraping using VBA.pdf	FILE	350825	C:\Users\deepa\Documents\My Creativity\Algorithm for Web Scraping using VBA.pdf	4/13/2020 18:26
Aparajita Drivers Licence v1.jpg	FILE	223874	C:\Users\deepa\Documents\My Creativity\Aparajita Drivers Licence v1.jpg	3/24/2020 13:05
artondenim.pdf	FILE	139315	C:\Users\deepa\Documents\My Creativity\artondenim.pdf	8/23/2020 14:59
bookmark.htm	FILE	61669	C:\Users\deepa\Documents\My Creativity\bookmark.htm	7/1/2020 13:44
Camera excel with screenshot processing.xlsm	FILE	60534	C:\Users\deepa\Documents\My Creativity\Camera excel with screenshot processing.xlsm	5/8/2019 14:21
CheckWebPage.xlsm	FILE	52262	C:\Users\deepa\Documents\My Creativity\CheckWebPage.xlsm	4/10/2020 9:48

5.3 CONCLUSION

This chapter helps you understand files and how to work with them in Excel VBA.

Manipulating files through a program enables you to maximize the automation opportunities in Excel and use them for several business scenarios.

This introductory concept is important since files still form a fundamental basis of exchanging information.

You also learnt the following:

- The DIR command
- Open and Close commands
- Recursion
- The MOD function
- Application Status Bar
- File Save As
- OnError Command
- Working with a File object

Here is an exercise for you.

Can you add a small enhancement to this program so that the user can enter a range of dates and receive a list of all files that were modified in that specified period?

6 Merging Sheets

Combine Multiple Workbooks of the Same Format into One Workbook Automatically

Spreadsheets are great to enforce a template.

If you are requesting data from a diverse group of people, and you are interested in knowing and perhaps analyzing the data they provide, you must ensure that the items they provide are uniform. Otherwise, you spend a whole lot of time sifting through their records and figuring out how to stack everything up.

Here is an example.

You are working on a survey where you really want to know the number of shoes sold in the last month for 100 stores by color, size, and type. So you distribute a survey and ask each store to fill them out. You include a format as below to ensure uniformity:

STORE	TYPE	COLOR	SIZE	NUMBER SOLD

Soon you have a 100 entries in your email box. Assuming that no one slacked off, you have the data from 100 stores perfectly formatted, which looked like this for the first Street Store:

STORE	TYPE	COLOR	SIZE	NUMBER SOLD
First Street	Goofey	red	S	300
First Street	Goofey	blue	M	100
First Street	Goofey	green	L	200
First Street	Goofey	black	S	300
First Street	Goofey	navy	M	100

DOI: 10.1201/9781003214335-7

STORE	TYPE	COLOR	SIZE	NUMBER SOLD
First Street	Mickey	red	L	300
First Street	Mickey	blue	S	100
First Street	Mickey	green	M	200
First Street	Mickey	black	L	300
First Street	Wonderland	navy	S	300
First Street	Wonderland	red	M	100
First Street	Wonderland	blue	L	200

The second Street Store wasn't so lucky and their sales were summarized in only five lines:

STORE	TYPE	COLOR	SIZE	NUMBER SOLD
Second Street	Wonderland	red	S	100
Second Street	Sandy	blue	M	100
Second Street	Sandy	green	L	200
Second Street	Sandy	black	S	300
Second Street	Sandy	navy	M	100

Once you receive all the stores, you want to collate them into one spreadsheet. The manual steps to do that are the following:

Step 1: Open a new spreadsheet
Step 2: Copy store 1 from row 1
Step 3: Copy store 2 from row 13, but do not copy the header
Step 4: Copy store 3 from row 19 but do not copy header
:
:
Step 101: Save spreadsheet

The final worksheet looks something like this:

STORE	TYPE	COLOR	SIZE	NUMBER SOLD
First Street	Goofey	red	S	300
First Street	Goofey	blue	M	100
First Street	Goofey	green	L	200
First Street	Goofey	black	S	300
First Street	Goofey	navy	M	100
First Street	Mickey	red	L	300
First Street	Mickey	blue	S	100
First Street	Mickey	green	M	200
First Street	Mickey	black	L	300
First Street	Wonderland	navy	S	300
First Street	Wonderland	red	M	100
First Street	Wonderland	blue	L	200

STORE	TYPE	COLOR	SIZE	NUMBER SOLD
Second Street	Wonderland	red	S	100
Second Street	Sandy	blue	M	100
Second Street	Sandy	green	L	200
Second Street	Sandy	black	S	300
Second Street	Sandy	navy	M	100
Third Street	Wonderland	red	S	100
Third Street	Sandy	blue	M	100
Third Street	Sandy	green	L	200
Third Street	Sandy	black	S	300
Third Street	Sandy	navy	M	100
:				
:				
:				
100th Street	Sandy	black	S	350

Now this is quite a bit of work.

Imagine if the survey contained two sheets in the same book. Perhaps sheet 1 is shoes and sheet 2 is dresses.

The work now doubles.

What about more than two sheets?

You get the picture. This needs some sort of automation.

6.1   ALGORITHM FOR MERGING SHEETS

In the algorithmic world, the steps are very similar, but we can use simple loops to do what we are doing manually.

This would translate to a set of steps as below:

Step 1: Open a new spreadsheet
Step 2: Create the header row in every worksheet
Step 3: For each workbook from a store
       For each worksheet in the workbook
           Read rows 2 to last row that contains data
           Move this row to the current row
           Advance to next row
       Next worksheet
     Next workbook
Step 4: Save workbook

6.2   USER INTERFACE

Using this algorithm, we can reduce the steps significantly and we can use these steps to now write the program that can automate it.

Following is the code that can do this task.

First create a spreadsheet in which you will write the code.

Create the entries exactly as shown below.

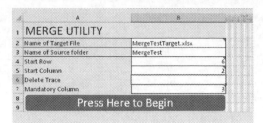

FIGURE 6.1   Merge utility.

Row 2 is where you would provide the name of the target file.

Row 3 is the source folder where you will store all the workbooks you received from the stores. Note that you should take care not to have any other file or else this would get picked up as well.

Row 4 is the uniform staring position for each source worksheet.

Row 5 is the start column of the data.

Row 6 is to indicate the deletion of traces created by the program. The program is written in such a way that the name of the source file is copied over in a far-away column just to ensure you can check which workbook the data came from.

Row 7 is a mandatory column where you will always expect data in the source sheets. If this column is blank for any row, then there are no data in that row. This is a rule we make up to ensure that we can systematically ensure all rows have been copied.

Rows 8 and 9 have a button that triggers the macro.

The button is just a shape that can be inserted using the following menu path.

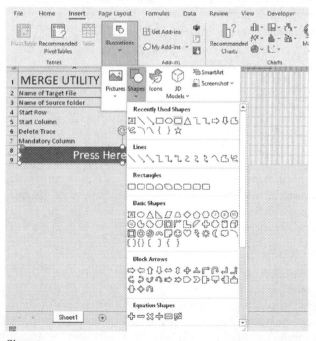

FIGURE 6.2   Shapes.

Once the button is created, you can assign the macro using a right mouse click as shown in Figure 6.3:

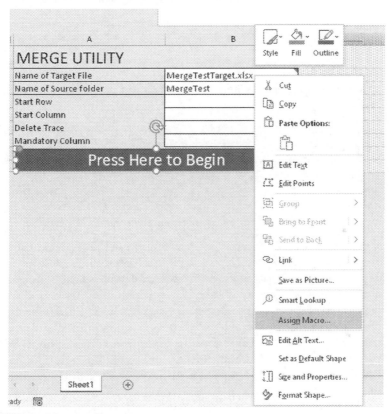

FIGURE 6.3 Macro assignment.

STEP 1—Initialize	Public Declare PtrSafe Function GetKeyboardState Lib "user32" (pbKeyState As Byte) As Long Public Declare PtrSafe Function GetAsyncKeyState Lib "User32.dll" (ByVal vKey As Long) As Long Public FirstTime As String Public CurrentWorkbookName As String Public ii As Double, kk As D18ouble, wb As Workbook, ws As Worksheet, jj As Double, NoData As Integer, B As String Public FirstRow, FirstColumn, MandatoryColumn, TraceColumn, RowMax, ColMax As Integer Public OverallTime As Double Public fileopenWb As Workbook, thisWb As Workbook Public fileopenTargetWb, parentWb As Workbook Public fileopenTargetWs As Worksheet, parentWs, thisWs As Worksheet Sub ExcelFileMerge()

| **STEP 1—Initialize continued** | ```
'
' ExcelFileMerge Macro
'

Dim NewBook As Workbook
Dim FSO As Object
Dim filepath As String
Dim rRange As Range
Dim A As String, Folder As String, FileName As String
NoData = 0
ii = 0
Set thisWb = ActiveWorkbook
Set parentWb = ActiveWorkbook
Set parentWs = ActiveSheet
filepathtarget = ActiveWorkbook.Path & "\" & Cells(2, 2)
RowMax = 100
ColMax = 22
TraceColumn = 100
x = Dir(filepathtarget)
FirstRow = Cells(4, 2)
FirstColumn = Cells(5, 2)
If FirstColumn <= 0 Then
    FirstColumn = 1
End If
MandatoryColumn = Cells(7, 2)
If MandatoryColumn < FirstColumn Then
    MandatoryColumn = FirstColumn
End If
``` Transferring these values from the selection screen in the previous page to a variable so that they can be used in the code |
| **STEP 2—prepare target** | ```
Do
    On Error GoTo continue
    Set fileopenTargetWb = Workbooks.Open(filepathtarget)
    Exit Do
continue:
    If x = "" Or Cells(2, 2) = "" Then
        MsgBox ("Please identify the target file")
        filepathtarget = Application.GetOpenFilename
    End If
    Set fileopenTargetWb = Workbooks.Open(filepathtarget)
Loop Until filepathtarget <> False

filePathTargetFuture = fileopenTargetWb.Path & "\" & fileopenTargetWb.Name & "-copy.xlsx"
fileopenTargetWb.SaveAs FileName:=filePathTargetFuture

x = parentWs.Cells(3, 2)
``` |

6.3   ERROR CORRECTION

This is an important step that has a nice error-correcting feature that you can use in many other programs. If the target file is not specified, then Cells(2,2) above will be blank. If it is specified, but is incorrect, then variable x will be blank.

If either of these two values are blank, then it means the code is heading for an error in subsequent "write" statements and will stop if the developer does not handle this condition appropriately.

Hence, this condition redirects the code to ask for a file name, starting with the "MsgBox".

The loop only executes once, because the variable "filepathtarget" is no longer false (or blank).

This type of DO…Loop iterative statement always executes at least once, because the condition check is at the end, unlike the For loop or the While loop.

```
                    If Right(parentWs.Cells(3, 2), 1) = "\" Then
                        Folder = ActiveWorkbook.Path & "\" & parentWs.Cells(3, 2)
                    Else
                        Folder = ActiveWorkbook.Path & "\" & parentWs.Cells(3, 2) & "\"
                        End If
STEP 3—main body of the program
                    x = Dir(Folder)

                    If Folder = "" Or x = "" Then
                        Call PickFolder(Folder)
                    End If
                    j = 0
                    Call GetFolderNames(Folder)
                    MsgBox ("Merge Complete. Be sure to save your file " & filePathTargetFuture)

                    If Left(parentWs.Cells(6, 2), 1) = "Y" Then
                        For Each Sheet In fileopenTargetWb.Worksheets
                            Sheet.Columns(ColMax + 1).EntireColumn.Delete
                        Next
                    End If

                    Application.StatusBar = False
                    fileopenTargetWb.Activate
                End Sub
```

6.4   HEAVY LIFTING

This is the part of the program that does all the heavy lifting.

The "call pickfolder" statement is activated to again do an error correction as in step 2. It checks if the source folder field was left blank or stated incorrectly. If either of those conditions is valid, then it presents the user with a dialog box that does not go away until the user has made a selection of the folder.

The "call getFolderNames" statement reads each file and copies each worksheet in each workbook over to the target workbook.

The subroutines called are here:

PickFolder	```
	Sub PickFolder(Folder)
	Dim fldr As FileDialog
	Dim sItem As String
	Set fldr = Application.FileDialog(msoFileDialogFolderPicker)
	With fldr
	   .Title = "Please Select a Folder by clicking (mandatory)"
	   .AllowMultiSelect = False
	   .InitialFileName = Application.DefaultFilePath
	   If .Show <> -1 Then GoTo NextCode
	   sItem = .SelectedItems(1)
	End With
	NextCode:
	If (InStr(1, sItem, "\") < Len(sItem)) Then
	   Folder = sItem & "\"
	Else
	   Folder = sItem
	End If
	Set fldr = Nothing
	End Sub
	``

GetFolderNames Initialize	```
	Sub GetFolderNames(Folder)
	   Dim FolderNames() As String
	   Dim SubFolders As Variant
	   Dim FileItem As Object
	   Dim SourceFolder As Object
	   FolderNameIndex = 0
	   Set fs = CreateObject("Scripting.FileSystemObject")
	   Set SourceFolder = fs.GetFolder(Folder)
	   For Each FileItem In SourceFolder.Files
	        On Error GoTo errorresume
	        A = FileItem.Name
	        Call PopulateRow(ii, A, Folder)
	        ii = ii + 1
	        Application.StatusBar = " Number of files " & (ii) & " complete "
	   Next
	   On Error GoTo errorresume
	   Exit Sub
	errorresume:
	   MsgBox ("Folder/File inaccessible! " & Folder & "\" & A)
	   k = k + 1
	End Sub
	``

```vba
Sub PopulateRow(ByRef ii As Double, ByVal B As String, ByVal Folder As String)
   OpenError = 1
   folderpath = Folder & B
    'open file
      On Error GoTo continue
      Set thisWb = Workbooks.Open(folderpath)
      OpenError = 0
continue:
   If OpenError = 1 Then
      MsgBox (B & " File cannot be opened")
   End If
x = 1
   If OpenError = 0 Then
      x = 1
         For Each Sheet In thisWb.Worksheets
            x = Sheet.Name
            y = WorksheetExists(x)
            If Sheet.Visible = True And WorksheetExists(x) Then
               On Error GoTo Nextsheet
               NumberOfRows1 = fileopenTargetWb.Sheets(Sheet.Name).Cells(Rows.
Count, FirstColumn).End(xlUp).Row
               NumberOfRows2 = FirstRow - 1
               NumberOfRows = WorksheetFunction.Max(NumberOfRows1,
NumberOfRows2)
                  If NumberOfRows < FirstRow - 1 Then
                     NumberOfRows = FirstRow - 1
                  End If
                  For i = FirstRow To FirstRow + RowMax
                     If thisWb.Sheets(Sheet.Name).Cells(i, MandatoryColumn) = "" Then
                        Exit For
                     End If
                     For j = FirstColumn To FirstColumn + ColMax
                        If thisWb.Sheets(Sheet.Name).Cells(i, j) <> "" Then
                           fileopenTargetWb.Sheets(Sheet.Name).Cells(NumberOfRows -
FirstRow + 1 + i, j) = thisWb.Sheets(Sheet.Name).Cells(i, j)
                        End If
                     Next j
                     fileopenTargetWb.Sheets(Sheet.Name).Cells(NumberOfRows -
FirstRow + 1 + i, ColMax + 1) = thisWb.Name
                  Next i
            End If
Nextsheet:
         Next
         thisWb.Close
      End If
End Sub
```

<table>
<tr><td rowspan="1">PickFile Initialize</td><td>

```
Sub PickFile(FileName)
      Dim fldr As FileDialog
      Dim sItem As String
      Set fldr = Application.FileDialog(msoFileDialogSaveAs)
      With fldr
        .Title = "Save as"
        .InitialFileName = "test.xlsx"
        .FilterIndex = 1
        If .Show <> 0 Then
           FileName = .SelectedItems(1)
           ActiveWorkbook.SaveAs FileName:=.SelectedItems(1)
        End If
      End With
End Sub
```

</td></tr>
</table>

6.5   THE PICKFILE SUBROUTINE

The PickFile is a subroutine that is executed in step 1 to save the target file. This is a technique to ensure that the target file is preserved, and the result of this program is a copy of what was provided as the target file. This has a unique advantage. Through this technique, you can do this process repetitively with the target file as one of the sources. If you have many files to merge, it can take some time to complete the operation. Breaking it up into chunks of ten files helps to ensure you do not run out of space and get an opportunity to save your work often.

A few more points about the PopulateRow subroutine.

A sheet is copied only if the sheet name matches the target. This avoids the issue of having extra sheets in your sources that the user might have created for their own calculation but is not relevant for your analysis. This is achieved by the statement "For Each Sheet In thisWb.Worksheets".

A piece of code needs to be called out for its ability to find the first blank row in the source file. The reason it is elegant is because it is so brief –

NumberOfRows1 = fileopenTargetWb.Sheets(Sheet.Name).Cells(Rows.Count,FirstColumn).End(x1Up).Row

End(x1up) positions the cursor on the last non-blank row.

6.6   CONCLUSION

Quite a few small techniques come in handy for a task as you try to automate it. This chapter discusses a macro that is extremely useful in many business situations. Although the task of copying cells to another sheet seems trivial, there are many intricate details that you must consider to successfully automate this process.

Some unique items you learnt in this chapter are:

- DO Loop
  - which is a special loop that executes at least once
- Workbook
  - opening and saving
- Worksheets
  - checking their names, copying from, copying to
- Application.FileDialogue
  - Open file
  - Save file
- OnError Goto Resume
  - handling errors

One exercise that you might like to work on:

How do you use this model to perform the exact opposite task of splitting a spreadsheet into multiple workbooks, so that each one is meant for a certain group identified by a key field in the workbook such as department, city, or state?

7 Introduction to Graphs
Create Your Own Interface Diagram Instantly

In real life, relationships between people can be good or bad. With data, relationships are always good. But they are of different types. Sometimes there is a pressing need to show these data relationships through a picture. As we know, a picture says a thousand words. That is why people love cartoons—if it is a good one, you can immediately uncover a 1,000-word story from it.

One such picture is a popular visual sometimes known as an interface diagram. It shows a source and a target and effectively lays out the direction and content of the data that flow from one to the other. For example, the inventory information in a warehouse flows into the order processing system so that it can order more parts when the inventory is depleted.

Converting this source-target information in a spreadsheet to a picture is time consuming. Wouldn't it be nice to automatically create it? With a little effort and a lot of imagination, you can do this through writing a macro that I am about to show you.

7.1 THE ALGORITHM

The algorithm is based on five steps. But before it can begin, the input must be in a certain format to recognize the source and target fields. To keep things really simple, we expect the first column to be the source, second column the target, and the third column a name for the arrow going from source to target. And this is put on a sheet called "Data".

	A	B	C
1	AD	SAP R3	Set up SSO for non-production
2	Applicant Insight	SAP R3	Feeds background status update
3	Bank of America	Transcentive	Employee Stock options export
4	Bright Horizon	SAP R3	@added from GDPR inventory lis
5	E&Y	SAP R3	E&Y -> WD monthly allowences
6	EDW	EDW	Active Directory Job for IDD P
7	EDW	EMS	Loads people data to EMS
8	EDW	SuccessFactors	Loads userid data to LMS
9	EDW	TeamConnect	Creates an Employee file to be
10	EDW	Transecure Travel	Populates the Transecure Trave

DOI: 10.1201/9781003214335-8

Step 1:

Review the "Data" list and create a list of entities in a tab called "Entities". An
entity is a thing with a unique name. So we basically go through columns A and
B and create a single list with all unique names.

Step 2:

Count up the number of connections for these entities and make a note of these as
shown below.

Entity	From Count	To Count	Total Count
AD	1		0
SAP R3		4	0
Applicant Insight	1		0
Bank of America	1		0
Transcentive		1	0
Bright Horizon	1		0
E&Y	1		0
EDW	5	1	0
EMS		1	0
SuccessFactors		1	0
TeamConnect		1	0
Transecure Travel		1	0

Step 3:

Draw the rectangles for each entity.

Step 4:

Draw the arrows for each pair of entity and set the labels to be the names in column
C of the data.

Step 5:

If the same "From" entity is connected to multiple "To" entities, or the same "To"
entity is connected to many "From" entities, this is not very easy to print on the
diagram. Create a special table for this during the previous steps. In this step, the
diagram is already drawn, so finish by printing the table that holds the multiple
source or multiple target labels.

For the example data above, this is what the diagram will look like.

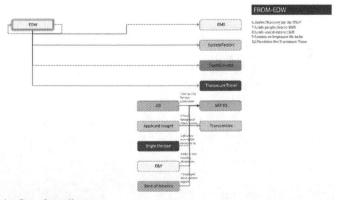

FIGURE 7.1   Interface diagram.

Here is the code:

STEP 1—initialization

```
Public Pair(500) As String
Public OldShapeBegin As Boolean
Public OldShapeEnd As Boolean
Public LinesInLabel(500) As Integer
Public LabelObject(500) As String
Public LabelObjectNumber As Integer
Public rng As Range, MyRct As Shape, WorkRange As Range
Public NumberOfEntities As Integer
Public NumberOfRows As Integer
Public RowsCompletedForCurrentMax As Integer
Public ToggleSwitch As Integer
Public CurrentSheetName As String
Sub Draw()
    Dim i As Integer, j As Integer, n As Integer, m As Integer
    Dim FromRange As Range, ToRange As Range
    LabelObjectNumber = 0
    Sheets("Diagram").Select
    NumberOfRows = CurrentSheet.Cells(Rows.Count, 1).End(xlUp).Row
    Dim Shp As Shape
    Dim arow As Integer, MaxCount As Integer, RowToGraph As Integer, ia As Integer
    For Each Shp In ActiveSheet.Shapes
        Shp.Delete
    Next Shp
    Dim DoneWithRow(500)
    For i = 1 To NumberOfRows
        DoneWithRow(i) = 0
    Next
    ColumnOffset = 1
    RowOffset = 0
    NumberOfRectangles = 0
    NextLeftShape = 1
    NextRightShape = 1
    j = 0
    k = 0
    Sheets("Entities").Select
    Cells.Select
    Selection.ClearContents
    Cells(1, 1) = "Entity"
    Cells(1, 2) = "From Count"
    Cells(1, 3) = "To Count"
    Cells(1, 4) = "Total Count"
```

STEP 1—check all sheets

```
' ** create all sheets required **
    Continue = InputBox("This worksheet must have the From Entity, To Entity and
Connection Name in the three initial columns without header. Continue?")
    If Left(Continue, 1) <> "Y" Then
       Exit Sub
    End If
    Dim sheet As Worksheet
    Dim CurrentSheet As Worksheet
    Set CurrentSheet = Application.ActiveSheet
    CurrentSheetName = ActiveSheet.Name

    FoundSheet = 0
    For Each sheet In ActiveWorkbook.Worksheets
    If sheet.Name = "Entities" Then
       FoundSheet = 1
       Exit For
    End If
    Next
    If FoundSheet = 0 Then
       Set sheet = ActiveWorkbook.Sheets.Add(After:=ActiveWorkbook.
Worksheets(ActiveWorkbook.Worksheets.Count))
       sheet.Name = "Entities"
    End If
       Worksheets("Entities").Cells(1, 1) = "Entity"
    Worksheets("Entities").Cells(1, 2) = "From Count"
    Worksheets("Entities").Cells(1, 3) = "To Count"
    Worksheets("Entities").Cells(1, 4) = "Total Count"
    FoundSheet = 0
    For Each sheet In ActiveWorkbook.Worksheets
    If sheet.Name = "IdenticalPairs" Then
       FoundSheet = 1
       Exit For
    End If
    Next
    If FoundSheet = 0 Then
    Set sheet = ActiveWorkbook.Sheets.Add(After:=ActiveWorkbook.
Worksheets(ActiveWorkbook.Worksheets.Count))
       sheet.Name = "IdenticalPairs"
    End If
    Worksheets("IdenticalPairs").Cells(1, 1) = "From"
    Worksheets("IdenticalPairs").Cells(1, 2) = "To"
    Worksheets("IdenticalPairs").Cells(1, 3) = "Additional Connection Name"
    FoundSheet = 0
    For Each sheet In ActiveWorkbook.Worksheets
    If sheet.Name = "Diagram" Then
       FoundSheet = 1
       Exit For
    End If
```

STEP 1 continued	Next
	If FoundSheet = 0 Then
	    Set sheet = ActiveWorkbook.Sheets.Add(After:=ActiveWorkbook.
	Worksheets(ActiveWorkbook.Worksheets.Count))
	    sheet.Name = "Diagram"
	End If
	' ** end create all sheets required

STEP 2	For i = 1 To NumberOfRows
	    Pair(i) = ""
	    FoundInstance = 0
	    For kk = 1 To k
	      If k > 1 And CurrentSheet.Cells(i, 1) = Worksheets("Entities").Cells(kk + 1, 1) Then
	        FoundInstance = 1
	        Worksheets("Entities").Cells(kk + 1, 2) = Worksheets("Entities").Cells(kk +
	        1, 2) + 1
	        Worksheets("Entities").Cells(kk + 1, 4) = Worksheets("Entities").Cells(kk +
	        1, 4) + 1
	        Exit For
	      Else
	        FoundInstance = 0
	      End If
	    Next
	    If FoundInstance = 0 Then
	      k = k + 1
	      Worksheets("Entities").Cells(k + 1, 1) = CurrentSheet.Cells(i, 1)
	      Worksheets("Entities").Cells(k + 1, 2) = 1
	      Worksheets("Entities").Cells(k + 1, 4) = 1
	    End If
	    FoundInstance = 0
	    For kk = 1 To k
	    If CurrentSheet.Cells(i, 2) = Worksheets("Entities").Cells(kk + 1, 1) Then
	      FoundInstance = 1
	      Worksheets("Entities").Cells(kk + 1, 3) = Worksheets("Entities").Cells(kk + 1, 3) + 1
	      Worksheets("Entities").Cells(kk + 1, 4) = Worksheets("Entities").Cells(kk + 1, 4) + 1
	      Exit For
	    Else
	      FoundInstance = 0
	    End If
	    Next
	    If FoundInstance = 0 Then
	  For i = k = k + 1
	      Worksheets("Entities").Cells(k + 1, 1) = CurrentSheet.Cells(i, 2)
	      Worksheets("Entities").Cells(k + 1, 3) = 1
	      Worksheets("Entities").Cells(k + 1, 4) = 1
	    End If
	  Next
	NumberOfEntities = Worksheets("Entities").Cells(Rows.Count, 1).End(xlUp).Row
	Sheets("IdenticalPairs").Select
	Cells.Select

| **STEP 2 continued** | ```
Selection.ClearContents
Cells(1, 1) = "From"
Cells(1, 2) = "To"
Cells(1, 3) = "Additional Connection Name"
CurrentSheet.Select
Range("D:D").Select
Selection.ClearContents
Sheets("Entities").Select
RowsCompletedForCurrentMax = 0
Call FindMax(arow, MaxCount)
Call FindRowToGraph(RowToGraph, ia, arow)
Previousarow = arow
HighestMaxCount = Worksheets("Entities").Cells(arow, 3).Value
ToggleSwitch = -1
PreviousToggleSwitch = ToggleSwitch
MaxNextLeftShape = 1
MaxNextRightSHape = 1
``` |
| **STEP 2 functions** | ```
Sub FindMax(arow As Integer, MaxCount As Integer)

        Set rng = Sheets("Entities").Range(Cells(2, 4), Cells(NumberOfEntities, 4))
        MaxCount = Application.WorksheetFunction.Max(rng)
        Set WorkRange = rng.Find(what:=MaxCount)
        arow = WorkRange.Row
        Worksheets("Entities").Cells(arow, 4).Value = 0
End Sub
Sub FindRowToGraph(RowToGraph As Integer, ia As Integer, arow As Integer)
        RowToGraph = 0

        For ia = 1 To NumberOfRows

            If Worksheets("Entities").Cells(arow, 1) = Sheets(CurrentSheetName).
Cells(ia, 2) And Sheets(CurrentSheetName).Cells(ia, 4) <> "Y" Then
            RowToGraph = ia
            ToggleSwitch = -1
            Sheets(CurrentSheetName).Cells(ia, 4) = "Y"
            Exit For
          End If
        Next
        If RowToGraph = 0 Then
          For ia = 1 To NumberOfRows
            If Worksheets("Entities").Cells(arow, 1) = Sheets(CurrentSheetName).
Cells(ia, 1) And Sheets(CurrentSheetName).Cells(ia, 4) <> "Y" Then
                RowToGraph = ia
                ToggleSwitch = 1
                Sheets(CurrentSheetName).Cells(ia, 4) = "Y"
                Exit For
            End If
          Next
        End If
End Sub
``` |

```
Sheets("Diagram").Select
While MaxCount > 0
  'For i = 1 To NumberOfRows
    ' poll the entities sheet to see which one has max count of connections. start there,
and then go to the next, etc
    i = RowToGraph
    If (Previousarow <> arow Or PreviousToggleSwitch <> ToggleSwitch) And
MaxCount > 5 Then
        'RowsCompletedForCurrentMax = 0
        If ToggleSwitch = -1 Then
          HighestMaxCount = Worksheets("Entities").Cells(arow, 2).Value
        Else
          HighestMaxCount = Worksheets("Entities").Cells(arow, 3).Value
        End If
        If NextLeftShape > 1 Then
          If ColumnOffset <> 36 Then
            If MaxNextLeftShape > NextLeftShape Then
              MaxNextLeftShape = NextLeftShape
            End If
            NextLeftShape = 1
            If MaxNextRightSHape > NextRightShape Then
              MaxNextRightSHape = NextRightShape
            End If
            NextRightShape = 1
            ColumnOffset = ColumnOffset + 12
          Else
          ' this part of the code is disabled now since columnoffset will never be
equal to 36.
          ' But can be changed to fit in a less wide and more tall format
          ColumnOffset = 0
          If MaxNextLeftShape > NextLeftShape Then
            MaxNextLeftShape = NextLeftShape
          End If
          NextLeftShape = 1
          If MaxNextRightSHape > NextRightShape Then
            MaxNextRightSHape = NextRightShape
        End If
        NextRightShape = 1
        RowOffset = RowOffset + 7 * MaxNextRightSHape
        End If
      End If
    End If
End If
    k = 6 * NextLeftShape + 2 + RowOffset
    l = 1 + ColumnOffset
    m = k + 2
    n = 4 + ColumnOffset
    OldShapeBegin = True
    Label = CurrentSheet.Cells(i, 1)
    If Label <> "" Then
      If Not ShapeExists(Label) Then
```

STEP 3 & 4

```
              OldShapeBegin = False
              'End If
              NumberOfRectangles = NumberOfRectangles + 1
              NextLeftShape = NextLeftShape + 1
              Call DrawRectangle(k, l, m, n, Label, i, "Begin") 'Draw first box
          End If
      End If
      k = 6 * NextRightShape + 2 + RowOffset
      l = 7 + ColumnOffset
      m = k + 2
      n = 10 + ColumnOffset
      OldShapeEnd = True
      Label = CurrentSheet.Cells(i, 2)
      If Label <> "" Then
          If Not ShapeExists(Label) Then
              OldShapeEnd = False
              'End If
              NumberOfRectangles = NumberOfRectangles + 1
              NextRightShape = NextRightShape + 1
              If OldShapeBegin Then
                  NextLeftShape = NextLeftShape + 1
              End If
              Call DrawRectangle(k, l, m, n, Label, i, "End") 'Draw second box
          End If
      End If
      Call DrawArrow(i) 'Draw the arrow
      Previousarow = arow
      PreviousToggleSwitch = ToggleSwitch
      Call FindRowToGraph(RowToGraph, ia, arow)
      If RowToGraph = 0 Then
          Sheets("Entities").Select
          While RowToGraph = 0 And MaxCount > 0
              Call FindMax(arow, MaxCount)
              Call FindRowToGraph(RowToGraph, ia, arow)
          Wend
      End If
      Sheets("Diagram").Select
      'Next
  Wend
```

```
Sub DrawArrow(ByVal i As Integer)
    If Sheets(CurrentSheetName).Cells(i, 3).Value = "" Then
        Sheets(CurrentSheetName).Cells(i, 3).Value = "BLANK!"
    End If
    If Sheets(CurrentSheetName).Cells(i, 3).Value = Sheets(CurrentSheetName).
Cells(i, 2).Value Then
        Sheets(CurrentSheetName).Cells(i, 3).Value = Sheets(CurrentSheetName).
Cells(i, 2).Value & "-" & i
    End If
    If Sheets(CurrentSheetName).Cells(i, 3).Value = Sheets(CurrentSheetName).
Cells(i, 1).Value Then
```

```
              Sheets(CurrentSheetName).Cells(i, 3).Value = Sheets(CurrentSheetName).
Cells(i, 1).Value & "-" & i
        End If
        FoundPair = 0
        For j = 1 To NumberOfRows
          If Pair(j) <> "" Then
            If Pair(j) = Sheets(CurrentSheetName).Cells(i, 1).Value &
Sheets(CurrentSheetName).Cells(i, 2).Value Then
              FoundPair = j
            Exit For
            End If
          End If
        Next
        ' *** Left Shape has 1 space before its name, Right Shape has 2 ***
        If OldShapeBegin And FoundPair = 0 Then
          ActiveSheet.Shapes(Sheets(CurrentSheetName).Cells(i, 1).Value).Select
          If Left((Selection.ShapeRange(1).TextFrame2.TextRange.Characters.Text),
2) = " " Then
            FromConnection = 1
            CircleLeft = Selection.ShapeRange(1).Left
            CircleTop = Selection.ShapeRange(1).Top
          Else
            FromConnection = 3
            adjustment = 10
          End If
        Else
          FromConnection = 4
        End If
        If OldShapeEnd And FoundPair = 0 Then
          ActiveSheet.Shapes(Sheets(CurrentSheetName).Cells(i, 1).Value).Select
          If Left((Selection.ShapeRange(1).TextFrame2.TextRange.Characters.Text),
2) = " " Then
            ToConnection = 2
          Else
            ToConnection = 2
          End If
        Else
            ToConnection = 2
        End If
If (OldShapeBegin Or OldShapeEnd) And FoundPair = 0 Then
        If FromConnection = 1 Then
        'add circle
        ActiveSheet.Shapes.AddShape(msoShapeOval, CircleLeft + 250, CircleTop, 16.5,
21).Select
        Selection.ShapeRange.Fill.Visible = msoFalse
        Selection.ShapeRange.Name = "Oval-" & i
        'add connection from 1st box to circle
        ActiveSheet.Shapes.AddConnector(msoConnectorElbow, 1, 1, 1, 1).Select
        ArrowColor = (20 + 5 * 1) Mod 255
```

STEP 3 & 4—draw arrow function continued 1

```
        With Selection.ShapeRange.Line
          .BeginArrowheadStyle = msoArrowheadNone
          .EndArrowheadStyle = msoArrowheadOpen
          .Weight = 2.75
          .Transparency = 0.5
          'color arrow
          .ForeColor.RGB = RGB(ArrowColor, ArrowColor, ArrowColor) 'black
        End With
          Selection.ShapeRange.ConnectorFormat.BeginConnect ActiveSheet.
Shapes(Sheets(CurrentSheetName).Cells(i, 1).Value), FromConnection
          Selection.ShapeRange.ConnectorFormat.EndConnect ActiveSheet.
Shapes("Oval-" & i), 5
          'add connection from circle to 2nd box below
          End If
          ActiveSheet.Shapes.AddConnector(msoConnectorElbow, 1, 1, 1, 1).Select
          'format line
          ArrowColor = (20 + 5 * 1) Mod 255
          'ArrowColor = (20 + 5 * i) Mod 255
        With Selection.ShapeRange.Line
          .BeginArrowheadStyle = msoArrowheadNone
          .EndArrowheadStyle = msoArrowheadOpen
          .Weight = 2.75
            .Transparency = 0.5
          'color arrow
          .ForeColor.RGB = RGB(ArrowColor, ArrowColor, ArrowColor) 'black
        End With
        Selection.ShapeRange.ZOrder msoSendToBack
        Selection.ShapeRange.Name = Sheets(CurrentSheetName).Cells(i, 3).Value & "<"
        If FromConnection = 1 Then
            Selection.ShapeRange.ConnectorFormat.BeginConnect ActiveSheet.
Shapes("Oval-" & i), 8
        Else
            Selection.ShapeRange.ConnectorFormat.BeginConnect ActiveSheet.
Shapes(Sheets(CurrentSheetName).Cells(i, 1).Value), FromConnection
        End If
        Selection.ShapeRange.ConnectorFormat.EndConnect ActiveSheet.
Shapes(Sheets(CurrentSheetName).Cells(i, 2).Value), ToConnection
            'Selection.ShapeRange.ConnectorFormat.EndConnect ActiveSheet.
Shapes(Sheets(CurrentSheetName).Cells(i, 1).Value & "/" & i), 2
            'Selection.ShapeRange.RerouteConnections
      End If
      ' *** the code here was to connect using connector rectangles, if required.
Currently not using rectangle
      If Not OldShapeBegin And Not OldShapeEnd And FoundPair = 0 Then
          ActiveSheet.Shapes.AddConnector(msoConnectorElbow, 1, 1, 1, 1).Select
            'format line
          'ArrowColor = (20 + 5 * i) Mod 255
          ArrowColor = (20 + 5 * 1) Mod 255
          With Selection.ShapeRange.Line
```

```
        .BeginArrowheadStyle = msoArrowheadNone
        .EndArrowheadStyle = msoArrowheadOpen
        .Weight = 2.75
        .Transparency = 0.5
        'color arrow
        .ForeColor.RGB = RGB(ArrowColor, ArrowColor, ArrowColor) 'black
    End With
        Selection.ShapeRange.ZOrder msoSendToBack
        Selection.ShapeRange.Name = Sheets(CurrentSheetName).Cells(i, 3).Value
        ActiveSheet.Shapes(Sheets(CurrentSheetName).Cells(i, 1).Value & "/" & i), 1
        Selection.ShapeRange.ConnectorFormat.BeginConnect ActiveSheet.
Shapes(Sheets(CurrentSheetName).Cells(i, 1).Value), 4
        Selection.ShapeRange.ConnectorFormat.EndConnect ActiveSheet.
Shapes(Sheets(CurrentSheetName).Cells(i, 2).Value), 2
    End If
    ' ***
    If Sheets(CurrentSheetName).Cells(i, 1) = Sheets(CurrentSheetName).Cells(i,
2) Then
        adjustment = -0.2
        Selection.ShapeRange.Adjustments.Item(1) = adjustment
    End If
    LabelRow = Range(ActiveSheet.Shapes(Sheets(CurrentSheetName).Cells(i, 1).
Value).TopLeftCell.Address).Row
    LabelCol = Range(ActiveSheet.Shapes(Sheets(CurrentSheetName).Cells(i, 1).
Value).TopLeftCell.Address).Column + 4
    Dim rng As Range, MyRct As Shape
    Label = Sheets(CurrentSheetName).Cells(i, 1).Value & "-1"
    Label2 = Sheets(CurrentSheetName).Cells(i, 1).Value & "-2"
    If OldShapeBegin And FromConnection = 1 Then
        ' 2 rows up 4 columns left
        If ShapeExists(Label2) Then
            Selection.ShapeRange.TextFrame2.TextRange.Characters.Text = Selection.
ShapeRange.TextFrame2.TextRange.Characters.Text & Chr(10) & i & "." &
Sheets(CurrentSheetName).Cells(i, 3).Value
        For kk = 1 To LabelObjectNumber
            If LabelObject(kk) = Label2 Then
                LinesInLabel(kk) = LinesInLabel(kk) + 1
            End If
        Next
    Else
        LabelObjectNumber = LabelObjectNumber + 1
        LinesInLabel(LabelObjectNumber) = 1
        LabelObject(LabelObjectNumber) = Label2
        Set rng = Range(Cells(LabelRow - 2, LabelCol - 4), Cells(LabelRow,
LabelCol - 3))
        With rng
            Set MyRct = ActiveSheet.Shapes.AddLabel(msoTextOrientationHorizontal,
.Left, .Top, .Width, .Height)
            MyRct.Name = Sheets(CurrentSheetName).Cells(i, 1).Value & "-2"
```

<table>
<tr>
<td rowspan="2" style="writing-mode: vertical">STEP 3 & 4—draw arrow function continued 3</td>
<td>

```
            MyRct.TextFrame2.TextRange.Characters.Text = i & "." &
Sheets(CurrentSheetName).Cells(i, 3).Value
            MyRct.TextFrame2.TextRange.Characters.Font.Size = 6
            MyRct.TextFrame2.VerticalAnchor = msoAnchorBottom
            MyRct.TextFrame2.TextRange.ParagraphFormat.Alignment = msoAlignLeft
            MyRct.TextFrame2.TextRange.Characters.Font.Fill.ForeColor.
RGB = RGB(255, 0, 0)
            MyRct.TextFrame2.AutoSize = msoAutoSizeShapeToFitText
          End With
        End If
      Else
      If ShapeExists(Label) Then
        Selection.ShapeRange.TextFrame2.TextRange.Characters.Text = Selection.
ShapeRange.TextFrame2.TextRange.Characters.Text & Chr(10) & i & "." &
Sheets(CurrentSheetName).Cells(i, 3).Value
          For kk = 1 To LabelObjectNumber
            If LabelObject(kk) = Label Then
            LinesInLabel(kk) = LinesInLabel(kk) + 1
          End If
        Next
      Else
        LabelObjectNumber = LabelObjectNumber + 1
        LinesInLabel(LabelObjectNumber) = 1
        LabelObject(LabelObjectNumber) = Label
        Set rng = Range(Cells(LabelRow, LabelCol), Cells(LabelRow + 2, LabelCol + 1))
        With rng
          Set MyRct = ActiveSheet.Shapes.AddLabel(msoTextOrientationHorizontal,
.Left, .Top, .Width, .Height)
          MyRct.Name = Sheets(CurrentSheetName).Cells(i, 1).Value & "-1"
          MyRct.TextFrame2.TextRange.Characters.Text = i & "." &
Sheets(CurrentSheetName).Cells(i, 3).Value
          MyRct.TextFrame2.TextRange.Characters.Font.Size = 6
          MyRct.TextFrame2.VerticalAnchor = msoAnchorBottom
          MyRct.TextFrame2.TextRange.ParagraphFormat.Alignment = msoAlignLeft
          MyRct.TextFrame2.TextRange.Characters.Font.Fill.ForeColor.
RGB = RGB(255, 0, 0)
          MyRct.TextFrame2.AutoSize = msoAutoSizeShapeToFitText
        End With
      End If
    End If
    If FoundPair = 0 Then
      Pair(i) = Sheets(CurrentSheetName).Cells(i, 1).Value &
Sheets(CurrentSheetName).Cells(i, 2).Value
    Else
      j = Worksheets("IdenticalPairs").Cells(Rows.Count, 1).End(xlUp).Row + 1
    Worksheets("IdenticalPairs").Cells(j, 1).Value = Sheets(CurrentSheetName).Cells(i,
1).Value
      Worksheets("IdenticalPairs").Cells(j, 2).Value = Sheets(CurrentSheetName).
Cells(i, 2).Value
```

</td>
</tr>
</table>

STEP 3 & 4—draw arrow function continued 3

```
        Worksheets("IdenticalPairs").Cells(j, 3).Value = Sheets(CurrentSheetName).
Cells(i, 3).Value
        LabelToHighlight = Sheets(CurrentSheetName).Cells(FoundPair, 1).Value & "-1"
        On Error Resume Next
        ActiveSheet.Shapes.Range(Array(LabelToHighlight)).Select
        On Error Resume Next
        Selection.ShapeRange(1).Fill.ForeColor.RGB = RGB(255, 255, 0) 'yellow
highlight
        LabelToHighlight = Sheets(CurrentSheetName).Cells(FoundPair, 1).Value & "-2"
        On Error Resume Next
        ActiveSheet.Shapes.Range(Array(LabelToHighlight)).Select
        On Error Resume Next
        Selection.ShapeRange(1).Fill.ForeColor.RGB = RGB(255, 255, 0) 'yellow
highlight
     End If
End Sub
        LabelObjectNumber = LabelObjectNumber + 1
        LinesInLabel(LabelObjectNumber) = 1
        LabelObject(LabelObjectNumber) = Label2
        Set rng = Range(Cells(LabelRow - 2, LabelCol - 4), Cells(LabelRow,
LabelCol - 3))
        With rng
           Set MyRct = ActiveSheet.Shapes.AddLabel(msoTextOrientationHorizontal,
.Left, .Top, .Width, .Height)
           MyRct.Name = Sheets(CurrentSheetName).Cells(i, 1).Value & "-2"
           MyRct.TextFrame2.TextRange.Characters.Text = i & "." &
Sheets(CurrentSheetName).Cells(i, 3).Value
           MyRct.TextFrame2.TextRange.Characters.Font.Size = 6
           MyRct.TextFrame2.VerticalAnchor = msoAnchorBottom
           MyRct.TextFrame2.TextRange.ParagraphFormat.Alignment = msoAlignLeft
           MyRct.TextFrame2.TextRange.Characters.Font.Fill.ForeColor.
RGB = RGB(255, 0, 0)
           MyRct.TextFrame2.AutoSize = msoAutoSizeShapeToFitText
        End With
     End If
   Else
     If ShapeExists(Label) Then
        Selection.ShapeRange.TextFrame2.TextRange.Characters.Text = Selection.
ShapeRange.TextFrame2.TextRange.Characters.Text & Chr(10) & i & "." &
Sheets(CurrentSheetName).Cells(i, 3).Value
           For kk = 1 To LabelObjectNumber
             If LabelObject(kk) = Label Then
                LinesInLabel(kk) = LinesInLabel(kk) + 1
             End If
           Next
        Else
           LabelObjectNumber = LabelObjectNumber + 1
           LinesInLabel(LabelObjectNumber) = 1
           LabelObject(LabelObjectNumber) = Label
```

```
            Set rng = Range(Cells(LabelRow, LabelCol), Cells(LabelRow + 2,
LabelCol + 1))
            With rng
            Set MyRct = ActiveSheet.Shapes.AddLabel(msoTextOrientationHorizontal,
.Left, .Top, .Width, .Height)
            MyRct.Name = Sheets(CurrentSheetName).Cells(i, 1).Value & "-1"
            MyRct.TextFrame2.TextRange.Characters.Text = i & "." &
Sheets(CurrentSheetName).Cells(i, 3).Value
            MyRct.TextFrame2.TextRange.Characters.Font.Size = 6
            MyRct.TextFrame2.VerticalAnchor = msoAnchorBottom
            MyRct.TextFrame2.TextRange.ParagraphFormat.Alignment = msoAlignLeft
            MyRct.TextFrame2.TextRange.Characters.Font.Fill.ForeColor.
RGB = RGB(255, 0, 0)
            MyRct.TextFrame2.AutoSize = msoAutoSizeShapeToFitText
         End With
      End If
    End If
    If FoundPair = 0 Then
      Pair(i) = Sheets(CurrentSheetName).Cells(i, 1).Value &
Sheets(CurrentSheetName).Cells(i, 2).Value
    Else
      j = Worksheets("IdenticalPairs").Cells(Rows.Count, 1).End(xlUp).Row + 1
      Worksheets("IdenticalPairs").Cells(j, 1).Value = Sheets(CurrentSheetName).
Cells(i, 1).Value
      Worksheets("IdenticalPairs").Cells(j, 2).Value = Sheets(CurrentSheetName).
Cells(i, 2).Value
      Worksheets("IdenticalPairs").Cells(j, 3).Value = Sheets(CurrentSheetName).
Cells(i, 3).Value
      LabelToHighlight = Sheets(CurrentSheetName).Cells(FoundPair, 1).Value & "-1"
      On Error Resume Next
      ActiveSheet.Shapes.Range(Array(LabelToHighlight)).Select
      On Error Resume Next
      Selection.ShapeRange(1).Fill.ForeColor.RGB = RGB(255, 255, 0) 'yellow
highlight
      LabelToHighlight = Sheets(CurrentSheetName).Cells(FoundPair, 1).Value & "-2"
      On Error Resume Next
      ActiveSheet.Shapes.Range(Array(LabelToHighlight)).Select
      On Error Resume Next
      Selection.ShapeRange(1).Fill.ForeColor.RGB = RGB(255, 255, 0) 'yellow
highlight
    End If
    End Sub
Sub DrawRectangle(ByVal i As Integer, ByVal j As Integer, ByVal m As Integer, ByVal
n As Integer, ByVal Label, ByVal RowNum As Integer, ByVal BeginOrEnd As String)
    Dim rng As Range, MyRct As Shape
    If (BeginOrEnd = "Begin" And OldShapeBegin) Or (BeginOrEnd = "End" And
OldShapeEnd) Then
       Set rng = Range(Cells(i, j), Cells(m, n))
       With rng
```

STEP 3 & 4—draw rectangle function

```
            Set MyRct = ActiveSheet.Shapes.AddShape(msoShapeRoundedRectangle,
    .Left, .Top, .Width, .Height)
            MyRct.Fill.Visible = msoFalse
            MyRct.Line.ForeColor.SchemeColor = 23
            MyRct.Line.Weight = 2.7
          'MyRct.Name = Label & "/" & RowNum
            MyRct.Name = Label
            MyRct.ScaleHeight 0.01, msoFalse, msoScaleFromTopLeft
             'MyRct.TextEffect.Text = Label
             'MyRct.TextEffect.FontSize = 20
             'MyRct.TextFrame.HorizontalAlignment = xlHAlignCenter
             'MyRct.TextFrame.VerticalAlignment = xlVAlignCenter
             'MyRct.TextFrame.Characters.Font.Color = RGB(20, 20, 20)
         End With
      Else
        If BeginOrEnd = "Begin" Then
           LabelPadding = " "
        Else
           LabelPadding = " "
        End If
         Set rng = Range(Cells(i, j), Cells(m, n))
         With rng
            Set MyRct = ActiveSheet.Shapes.AddShape(msoShapeRoundedRectangle,
    .Left, .Top, .Width, .Height)
            MyRct.Fill.ForeColor.SchemeColor = 33 + (i Mod 20)
            MyRct.Line.ForeColor.SchemeColor = 23
            MyRct.Name = Label
            MyRct.TextEffect.Text = LabelPadding & Label
            MyRct.TextEffect.FontSize = 20
            MyRct.TextFrame.HorizontalAlignment = xlHAlignCenter
            MyRct.TextFrame.VerticalAlignment = xlVAlignCenter
            MyRct.TextFrame.Characters.Font.Color = RGB(20, 20, 20)
         End With
      End If
   End Sub
   Function ShapeExists(Label)
      Dim ashp As Shape
      On Error GoTo error_handler:
      ShapeExists = True
      ActiveSheet.Shapes(Label).Select
      Exit Function
   error_handler:
      ShapeExists = False
   End Function
```

<table>
<tr><td rowspan="1">STEP 5</td><td>

```
    For i = 1 To LabelObjectNumber
      If LinesInLabel(i) > 3 Then
        n = n + 2
          Set rng = Range(Cells(2, n), Cells(2, n + 1))
          With rng
            Set MyRct = ActiveSheet.Shapes.AddLabel(msoTextOrientationHorizontal,
.Left, .Top, .Width, .Height)
            MyRct.Name = "Legend-" & i
            MyRct.TextFrame2.TextRange.Characters.Text = "FROM-"
&          Mid(LabelObject(i), 1, InStr(LabelObject(i), "-") - 1)
            MyRct.TextFrame2.TextRange.Characters.Font.Size = 10
            MyRct.TextFrame2.VerticalAnchor = msoAnchorBottom
            MyRct.TextFrame2.TextRange.ParagraphFormat.
Alignment = msoAlignLeft
            MyRct.TextFrame2.TextRange.Characters.Font.Fill.ForeColor.
RGB = RGB(255, 0, 0)
              MyRct.TextFrame2.AutoSize = msoAutoSizeShapeToFitText
              MyRct.Fill.ForeColor.RGB = RGB(50, 50, 0) ' highlight
              MyRct.Line.ForeColor.RGB = RGB(20, 20, 20)
          End With
        ActiveSheet.Shapes.Range(Array("Legend-" & i)).Select
        LegendLeft = Selection.ShapeRange.Left
        LegendTop = Selection.ShapeRange.Top
        ActiveSheet.Shapes.Range(Array(LabelObject(i))).Select
        Selection.ShapeRange.Left = LegendLeft + 0
        Selection.ShapeRange.Top = LegendTop + 35
        ActiveSheet.Shapes.Range(Array(Mid(LabelObject(i), 1, InStr(LabelObject(i), "-")
- 1))).Select
        Selection.ShapeRange.Line.Style = msoLineThickBetweenThin
        Selection.ShapeRange.Line.Weight = 10
      End If
        Next
      :
      :
End Sub 'Draw
```

</td></tr>
</table>

7.2   CONCLUSION

This chapter discusses simple ways to automate drawing of pictures using Microsoft's drawing tool that is embedded in Excel.

The tools explored here allow you to:

- Add worksheets in a workbook
- Control a shape such as square, rectangle, or circle
- Draw arrows
- Connect two shapes with arrows
- Change the weights of arrows

- Change fill colors
- Change outline colors
- Write text in shapes
- Highlight text in shapes
- Change the font of a text
- Check for the existence of a shape
- Provide a legend automatically
- Move shapes to a different part of the spreadsheet

A problem that you can work on your own –

Now that you know how to draw these shapes and place them on a spreadsheet, can you write some code to draw a floor plan of a two-bedroom house if you are given the dimensions? Something like an HGTV Design art that famous interior designers use?

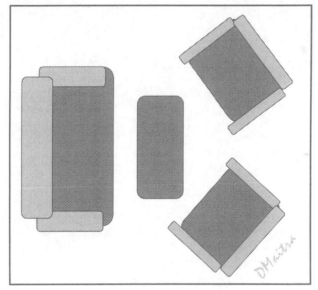

FIGURE 7.2   Drawing room.

8 Shaping up

Analyze a Picture and Document Its Components in Text

Sometimes we are faced with the opposite problem of what we saw in Chapter 6. We have a beautiful visual which lays it all out. But someone needs it in a spreadsheet form. This is especially useful for auditors who are trying to review a diagram for accuracy and completeness. Getting it on a spreadsheet opens up many possibilities of checking certain attributes of the data automatically that can otherwise only be verified through visual examination. For example, if we know that all process names must exceed ten characters, then it would be very beneficial to change the processes in a diagram to a spreadsheet in a long list and apply a formula to test if any of the process names exceeds ten characters. If we did not do that then the only way would be to pore over the diagram and count the letters manually in each process box.

This chapter is going to show you how you can do this conversion—from diagram to spreadsheet—so that you can apply your own formulas to the result when required.

8.1 THE ALGORITHM

The program is developed in three steps.

Step 1.
Collect all the different types of shapes that are possible on Excel. Since Excel uses a tool called MSDraw, it is easy to get this list from the Microsoft website. Shape is an object and there are two attributes that are essential in discovering them. These are Shape Type and AutoShape Type. The second attribute is really a qualifier of a shape that is already defined to be an AutoShape (Shape Type = "AutoShape"). Shapes can be of many types such as line, arrow, connections, pictures, comments, and so on. AutoShapes are those that have the ability to house text inside them and grow in size as required to fit this text—think rectangle, oval, triangle, etc.

DOI: 10.1201/9781003214335-9

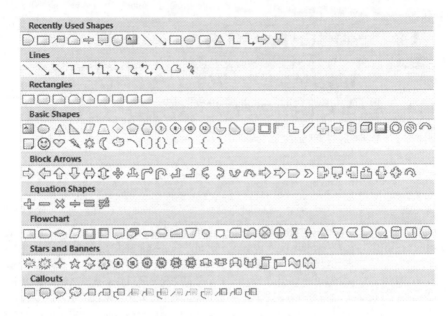

FIGURE 8.1 Shapes.

The picture above is a typical view of shapes that are available in MSDraw. Each one has a name and this is what we need to capture in a constant table (array).

Step 2.
The diagram needs to be read and each item analyzed for its attributes. Once analyzed, the items need to be recorded in the spreadsheet in their appropriate columns.

Step 3.
This last step is required to deal with shapes that are groups. MSDraw provides a feature of combining multiple shapes and calling them a "group". A "group" needs to be "ungrouped" and its components separately listed in the spreadsheet.

See this example below of a diagram.

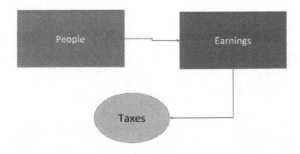

FIGURE 8.2 Example MSDraw diagram.

8.2   LIST OF SHAPES

This program will create a list of these objects in the format below.

AutoShape Type	Type	Name	Label
msoShapeRectangle	msoAutoShape	Rectangle 1	People
msoShapeRectangle	msoAutoShape	Rectangle 260	Earnings
msoShapeMixed	msoAutoShape	Elbow Connector 5	
msoShapeOval	msoAutoShape	Oval 6	Taxes
msoShapeMixed	msoAutoShape	Elbow Connector 261	

Creating a list like this is very useful when you are specifically looking for items in a complex diagram, or you simply want to create some documentation and want to make sure you are not missing an entity in your thesis or spell a word incorrectly.

Here is the code.

```
Public msoShapeTypeName As Variant
Public msoShapeTypeValue As Variant
Public msoShapeTypeDescription As Variant
Public msoAutoShapeTypeName() As String
Public msoAutoShapeTypeValue() As String
Public msoAutoShapeTypeDescription() As String
Public k As Integer
Sub ListShapes()
msoShapeTypeName = Array("Name", "mso3DModel", "msoAutoShape",
"msoCallout", "msoCanvas", "msoChart", "msoComment", "msoContentApp",
"msoDiagram", "msoEmbeddedOLEObject", "msoFormControl", "msoFreeform",
"msoGraphic", "msoGroup", "msoIgxGraphic", "msoInk", "msoInkComment",
"msoLine", "msoLinked3DModel", "msoLinkedGraphic", "msoLinkedOLEObject",
"msoLinkedPicture", "msoMedia", "msoOLEControlObject", "msoPicture",
"msoPlaceholder", "msoScriptAnchor", "msoShapeTypeMixed", "msoTable",
"msoTextBox", "msoTextEffect", "msoWebVideo")
msoShapeTypeValue = Array("Value", "30", "1", "2", "20", "3", "4", "27", "21", "7",
"8", "5", "28", "6", "24", "22", "23", "9", "31", "29", "10", "11", "16", "12", "13",
"14", "18", "-2", "19", "17", "15", "26")
msoShapeTypeDescription = Array("Description", "3D model", "AutoShape",
"Callout", "Canvas", "Chart", "Comment", "Content Office Add-in", "Diagram",
"Embedded OLE object", "Form control", "Freeform", "Graphic", "Group", "SmartArt
graphic", "Ink", "Ink comment", "Line", "Linked 3D model", "Linked graphic",
"Linked OLE object", "Linked picture", "Media", "OLE control object", "Picture",
"Placeholder", "Script anchor", "Mixed shape type", "Table", "Text box", "Text
effect", "Web video")
ConstText = _
"Name, msoShape10pointStar, msoShape12pointStar, msoShape16pointStar,
msoShape24pointStar, msoShape32pointStar, msoShape4pointStar,
msoShape5pointStar, msoShape6pointStar, msoShape7pointStar, msoShape8pointStar,
msoShapeActionButtonBackorPrevious, msoShapeActionButtonBeginning,
msoShapeActionButtonCustom,
```

msoShapeActionButtonDocument, msoShapeActionButtonEnd, msoShapeActionB
uttonForwardorNext, msoShapeActionButtonHelp, msoShapeActionButtonHome,
msoShapeActionButtonInformation, msoShapeActionButtonMovie,
msoShapeActionButtonReturn, msoShapeActionButtonSound, msoShapeArc,
msoShapeBalloon, msoShapeBentArrow, msoShapeBentUpArrow, msoShapeBevel,
msoShapeBlockArc, msoShapeCan, msoShapeChartPlus, msoShapeChartStar,
msoShapeChartX, msoShapeChevron, msoShapeChord, msoShapeCircularArrow,
msoShapeCloud, msoShapeCloudCallout, msoShapeCorner, msoShapeCornerTabs,
msoShapeCross, msoShapeCube, msoShapeCurvedDownArrow,
msoShapeCurvedDownRibbon, msoShapeCurvedLeftArrow,
msoShapeCurvedRightArrow, msoShapeCurvedUpArrow, msoShapeCurvedUpRibbon,
msoShapeD"
ConstText = ConstText & _
"ecagon, msoShapeDiagonalStripe, msoShapeDiamond, msoShapeDodecagon,
msoShapeDonut, msoShapeDoubleBrace, msoShapeDoubleBracket,
msoShapeDoubleWave, msoShapeDownArrow, msoShapeDownArrowCallout,
msoShapeDownRibbon, msoShapeExplosion1, msoShapeExplosion2,
msoShapeFlowchartAlternateProcess, msoShapeFlowchartCard,
msoShapeFlowchartCollate, msoShapeFlowchartConnector, msoShapeFlowchartData,
msoShapeFlowchartDecision, msoShapeFlowchartDelay, msoShapeFlowchartDi
rectAccessStorage, msoShapeFlowchartDisplay, msoShapeFlowchartDocument,
msoShapeFlowchartExtract, msoShapeFlowchartInternalStorage,
msoShapeFlowchartMagneticDisk, msoShapeFlowchartManualInput, mso
ShapeFlowchartManualOperation, msoShapeFlowchartMerge,
msoShapeFlowchartMultidocument, msoShapeFlowchartOfflineStorage, msoSh
apeFlowchartOffpageConnector, msoShapeFlowchartOr, msoShapeFlowchartP
redefinedProcess, msoShapeFlowchartPreparation, msoShapeFlowchartProcess,
msoShapeFlowchartPunchedTape, msoShapeFlowchartSequentialAccessStorage,
msoShapeFlowchartSort, msoShapeFlowchartStored"
ConstText = ConstText & _
"Data, msoShapeFlowchartSummingJunction, msoShapeFlowchartTerminator,
msoShapeFoldedCorner, msoShapeFrame, msoShapeFunnel, msoShapeGear6,
msoShapeGear9, msoShapeHalfFrame, msoShapeHeart, msoShapeHeptagon,
msoShapeHexagon, msoShapeHorizontalScroll, msoShapeIsoscelesTriangle,
msoShapeLeftArrow, msoShapeLeftArrowCallout, msoShapeLeftBrace,
msoShapeLeftBracket, msoShapeLeftCircularArrow, msoShapeLeftRightArrow,
msoShapeLeftRightArrowCallout, msoShapeLeftRightCircularArrow,
msoShapeLeftRightRibbon, msoShapeLeftRightUpArrow, msoShapeLeftUpArrow,
msoShapeLightningBolt, msoShapeLineCallout1, msoShapeLineCallout1AccentBar,
msoShapeLineCallout1BorderandAccentBar, msoShapeLineCallout1NoBorder,
msoShapeLineCallout2, msoShapeLineCallout2AccentBar, msoShape
LineCallout2BorderandAccentBar, msoShapeLineCallout2NoBorder,
msoShapeLineCallout3, msoShapeLineCallout3AccentBar, msoShapeLineCallout
3BorderandAccentBar, msoShapeLineCallout3NoBorder, msoShapeLineCallout4,
msoShapeLineCallout4AccentBar, msoShapeLineCallout4BorderandAccentBar,
msoShapeLin"
ConstText = ConstText & _

STEP 1 continued

"eCallout4NoBorder, msoShapeLineInverse, msoShapeMathDivide, msoShapeMathEqual, msoShapeMathMinus, msoShapeMathMultiply, msoShapeMathNotEqual, msoShapeMathPlus, msoShapeMixed, msoShapeMoon, msoShapeNonIsoscelesTrapezoid, msoShapeNoSymbol, msoShapeNotchedRightArrow, msoShapeNotPrimitive, msoShapeOctagon, msoShapeOval, msoShapeOvalCallout, msoShapeParallelogram, msoShapePentagon, msoShapePie, msoShapePieWedge, msoShapePlaque, msoShapePlaqueTabs, msoShapeQuadArrow, msoShapeQuadArrowCallout, msoShapeRectangle, msoShapeRectangularCallout, msoShapeRegularPentagon, msoShapeRightArrow, msoShapeRightArrowCallout, msoShapeRightBrace, msoShapeRightBracket, msoShapeRightTriangle, msoShapeRound1Rectangle, msoShapeRound2DiagRectangle, msoShapeRound2SameRectangle, msoShapeRoundedRectangle, msoShapeRoundedRectangularCallout, msoShapeSmileyFace, msoShapeSnip1Rectangle, msoShapeSnip2DiagRectangle, msoShapeSnip2SameRectangle, msoShapeSnipRoundRectangle, msoShapeSquareTabs, msoShapeStripedRightArrow, msoShapeSun, msoShapeSwooshArrow, msoShapeTear, msoSh"
ConstText = ConstText & _
"apeTrapezoid, msoShapeUpArrow, msoShapeUpArrowCallout, msoShapeUpDownArrow, msoShapeUpDownArrowCallout, msoShapeUpRibbon, msoShapeUTurnArrow, msoShapeVerticalScroll, msoShapeWave"
msoAutoShapeTypeName = Split(ConstText, ",")
ConstText = "Value, 149, 150, 94, 95, 96, 91, 92, 147, 148, 93, 129, 131, 125, 134, 132, 130, 127, 126, 128, 136, 133, 135, 25, 137, 41, 44, 15, 20, 13, 182, 181, 180, 52, 161, 60, 179, 108, 162, 169, 11, 14, 48, 100, 46, 45, 47, 99, 144, 141, 4, 146, 18, 27, 26, 104, 36, 56, 98, 89, 90, 62, 75, 79, 73, 64, 63, 84, 87, 88, 67, 81, 66, 86, 71, 72, 82, 68, 139, 74, 78, 65, 70, 61, 76, 85, 80, 83, 77, 69, 16, 158, 174, 172, 173, 159, 21, 145, 10, 102, 7, 34, 54, 31, 29, 176, 37, 57, 177, 140, 40, 43, 22, 109, 113, 121, 117, 110, 114, 122, 118, 111, 115, 123, 119, 112, 116, 124, 120, 183, 166, 167, 164, 165, 168, 163, -2, 24, 143, 19, 50, 138, 6, 9, 107, 2, 51, 142, 175, 28, 171, 39, 59, 1, 105, 12, 33, 53, 32, 30, 8, 151, 157, 152, 5, 106, 17, 155, 157, 156, 154, 170, 49, 23, 178, 160, 3, 35, 55, 38, 58, 97, 42, 101, 103"
msoAutoShapeTypeValue = Split(ConstText, ",")
ConstText = _
"Description#10-point star#12-point star#16-point star#24-point star#32-point star#4-point star#5-point star#6-point star#7-point star#8-point star#Back or Previous button. Supports mouse-click and mouse-over actions.#Beginning button. Supports mouse-click and mouse-over actions.#Button with no default picture or text. Supports mouse-click and mouse-over actions.#Document button. Supports mouse-click and mouse-over actions.#End button. Supports mouse-click and mouse-over actions.#Forward or Next button. Supports mouse-click and mouse-over actions.#Help button. Supports mouse-click and mouse-over actions.#Home button. Supports mouse-click and mouse-over actions.#Information button. Supports mouse-click and mouse-over actions.#Movie button. Supports mouse-click and mouse-over actions.#Return button. Supports mouse-click and mouse-over actions.#Sound button. Supports mouse-click and mouse-over actions.#Arc#Balloon#Block arrow that follows a curved 90-degree angle.#Block arrow that follows"
ConstText = ConstText & _

"a sharp 90-degree angle. Points up by default.#Bevel#Block arc#Can#Square divided vertically and horizontally into four quarters#Square divided into six parts along vertical and diagonal lines#Square divided into four parts along diagonal lines#Chevron#Circle with a line connecting two points on the perimeter through the interior of the circle; a circle with a chord#Block arrow that follows a curved 180-degree angle#Cloud shape#Cloud callout#Rectangle with rectangular-shaped hole.#Four right triangles aligning along a rectangular path; four 'snipped' corners.#Cross#Cube#Block arrow that curves down#Ribbon banner that curves down#Block arrow that curves left#Block arrow that curves right#Block arrow that curves up#Ribbon banner that curves up#Decagon#Rectangle with two triangles-shapes removed; a diagonal stripe#Diamond#Dodecagon#Donut#Double brace#Double bracket#Double wave#Block arrow that points down#Callout with arrow that points down#Ribbon banner with center area below ribbon ends"
ConstText = ConstText & _
"#Explosion#Explosion#Alternate process flowchart symbol#Card flowchart symbol#Collate flowchart symbol#Connector flowchart symbol#Data flowchart symbol#Decision flowchart symbol#Delay flowchart symbol#Direct access storage flowchart symbol#Display flowchart symbol#Document flowchart symbol#Extract flowchart symbol#Internal storage flowchart symbol#Magnetic disk flowchart symbol#Manual input flowchart symbol#Manual operation flowchart symbol#Merge flowchart symbol#Multi-document flowchart symbol#Offline storage flowchart symbol#Off-page connector flowchart symbol# Or flowchart symbol#Predefined process flowchart symbol#Preparation flowchart symbol#Process flowchart symbol#Punched tape flowchart symbol#Sequential access storage flowchart symbol#Sort flowchart symbol#Stored data flowchart symbol#Summing junction flowchart symbol#Terminator flowchart symbol#Folded corner#Rectangular picture frame#Funnel#Gear with six teeth#Gear with nine teeth#Half of a rectangular picture frame#Heart#Hep"
ConstText = ConstText & _
"tagon#Hexagon#Horizontal scroll#Isosceles triangle#Block arrow that points left#Callout with arrow that points left#Left brace#Left bracket#Circular arrow pointing counter-clockwise#Block arrow with arrowheads that point both left and right#Callout with arrowheads that point both left and right#Circular arrow pointing clockwise and counter-clockwise; a curved arrow with points at both ends#Ribbon with an arrow at both ends#Block arrow with arrowheads that point left, right, and up#Block arrow with arrowheads that point left and up#Lightning bolt#Callout with border and horizontal callout line#Callout with horizontal accent bar#Callout with border and horizontal accent bar#Callout with horizontal line#Callout with diagonal straight line#Callout with diagonal callout line and accent bar#Callout with border, diagonal straight line, and accent bar#Callout with no border and diagonal callout line#Callout with angled line#Callout with angled callout line and accent bar#Callout with border, a"
ConstText = ConstText & _
"ngled callout line, and accent bar#Callout with no border and angled callout line#Callout with callout line segments forming a U-shape#Callout with accent bar and callout line segments forming a U-shape#Callout with border, accent bar, and callout line segments forming a U-shape#Callout with no border and callout line segments forming a U-shape#Line inverse#Division symbol ö#Equivalence symbol = #Subtraction symbol -#Multiplication symbol x#Non-equivalence

STEP 1 continued	symbol?#Addition symbol +#Return value only; indicates a combination of the other states.#Moon#Trapezoid with asymmetrical non-parallel sides#No symbol#Notched block arrow that points right#Not supported#Octagon#Oval#Oval-shaped callout#Parallelogram#Pentagon#Circle ('pie') with a portion missing#Quarter of a circular shape#Plaque#Four quarter-circles defining a rectangular shape#Block arrows that point up, down, left, and right#Callout with arrows that point up, down, left, and right#Rectangle#Rectangular callout#Pentagon#Block ar" ConstText = ConstText & _ "row that points right#Callout with arrow that points right#Right brace#Right bracket#Right triangle#Rectangle with one rounded corner#Rectangle with two rounded corners, diagonally-opposed#Rectangle with two-rounded corners that share a side#Rounded rectangle#Rounded rectangle-shaped callout#Smiley face#Rectangle with one snipped corner#Rectangle with two snipped corners, diagonally-opposed#Rectangle with two snipped corners that share a side#Rectangle with one snipped corner and one rounded corner#Four small squares that define a rectangular shape#Block arrow that points right with stripes at the tail#Sun#Curved arrow#Water droplet#Trapezoid#Block arrow that points up#Callout with arrow that points up#Block arrow that points up and down#Callout with arrows that point up and down#Ribbon banner with center area above ribbon ends#Block arrow forming a U shape#Vertical scroll#Wave" msoAutoShapeTypeDescription = Split(ConstText, "#")

```
Dim sheet As Worksheet
Dim CurrentSheet As Worksheet
Set CurrentSheet = Application.ActiveSheet
FoundSheet = 0
For Each sheet In ActiveWorkbook.Worksheets
    If sheet.Name = "ShapeList" Then
        FoundSheet = 1
        Exit For
    End If
Next
If FoundSheet = 0 Then
    Set sheet = ActiveWorkbook.Sheets.Add(After:=ActiveWorkbook.
Worksheets(ActiveWorkbook.Worksheets.Count))
    sheet.Name = "ShapeList"
End If
Worksheets("ShapeList").Cells(1, 1) = "AutoShapeType"
Worksheets("ShapeList").Cells(1, 2) = "Type"
Worksheets("ShapeList").Cells(1, 3) = "Name"
Worksheets("ShapeList").Cells(1, 4) = "Label"
CurrentSheet.Select
'
    Dim shp As Shape
    kk = 1
    Sheets("ShapeList").Range("a2:d1000").Clear
    For Each shp In ActiveSheet.Shapes
      kk = kk + 1
      Call GetRows(kk, shp)
    Next shp
```

STEP 2

```
        For mm = 1 To kk
            If Left(Worksheets("ShapeList").Cells(mm, 3), 2) = "##" Then
                Worksheets("ShapeList").Cells(mm, 3) = Mid(Worksheets("ShapeList").
Cells(mm, 3), 3, 100)
                For Each shp In ActiveSheet.Shapes(Worksheets("ShapeList").Cells(mm,
3)).GroupItems
                    kk = kk + 1
                    Call GetRows(kk, shp)
                Next shp
            End If
        Next
End Sub
Sub GetRows(kk, shp)
        Worksheets("ShapeList").Cells(kk, 1) = shp.AutoShapeType
        k = UBound(msoAutoShapeTypeName)
        Call FindAutoShapeType(kk)

        Worksheets("ShapeList").Cells(kk, 2) = shp.Type

        k = UBound(msoShapeTypeName)
        Call FindShapeType(kk)

        Worksheets("ShapeList").Cells(kk, 3) = shp.Name
        On Error GoTo bypass
        a = shp.GroupItems.Count
        If a <> "" Then
        Worksheets("ShapeList").Cells(kk, 3) = "##" & shp.Name
        End If
        On Error GoTo bypass
        Worksheets("ShapeList").Cells(kk, 4) = shp.TextEffect.Text
        bypass:
          'Worksheets("ShapeList").Cells(kk, 4) = shp.GroupItems.Count
        Resume Next
End Sub
Sub FindShapeType(kk)
        FoundInstance = 0
        For i = 1 To k
        If k > 1 And msoShapeTypeValue(i) + 0 = Worksheets("ShapeList").Cells(kk,
2) Then
            FoundInstance = 1
            Worksheets("ShapeList").Cells(kk, 2) = msoShapeTypeName(i)
            Exit For
        Else
            FoundInstance = 0
        End If
      Next
End Sub
Sub FindAutoShapeType(kk)
        FoundInstance = 0
```

<table>
<tr><td rowspan="1">STEP 3 continued</td><td>

```
        For i = 1 To k
          If k > 1 And msoAutoShapeTypeValue(i) + 0 = Worksheets("ShapeList").
Cells(kk, 1) Then
            FoundInstance = 1
            Worksheets("ShapeList").Cells(kk, 1) = msoAutoShapeTypeName(i)
            Exit For
          Else
            FoundInstance = 0
          End If
        Next
End Sub
```

</td></tr>
</table>

8.3   CONCLUSION

In this chapter, instead of analyzing text to draw a graph, we analyzed a graph and developed its description in text form. This is beneficial when the original text that the graph was based upon is not available. This technique is also useful for data analytics—the text can be extended with other data points to develop intuitive conclusions about the scenario that the graph depicts. While there are many tools that provide insightful analysis based on data, there are very few that can analyze graphical inputs and provide textual inferences. Sometimes it is helpful even to count the number of arrows in a diagram, because it helps to corelate and confirm the contents of an intricate picture.

In this chapter you learned:

- Cataloguing shapes
- Recognizing types, names, and labels
- Working with groups

Here is a problem for you to work on your own.

Can you extend the code provided to count the number of rectangles, triangles, and circles in the diagram? And can you classify them by color—for example, three red circles, two green rectangles, and so on?

9 Real-Time Currency Conversion

An Introduction to Simple Web Scraping Techniques

There are two types of information one is accustomed to using these days—information at work that is required to do one's job and information at home to complete a personal chore. The former is mostly on spreadsheets—sales figures, targets, budgets, etc. The latter is mostly on the web—for example, where is the nearest gas station, when does my favorite Indian restaurant close, and so on.

What if I need both types at once? What if I am trying to compile a list of hotels within a five-mile radius of 40 different office locations in the United States for my company? In fact, most jobs that have even a small amount of research content involve pulling data from the web and compiling them for further analysis. A financial consultant may be looking at the exchange rates and compiling them every single day. A fund manager may be interested in a daily update of stock prices to analyze trends, etc.

The art of grabbing information from the web without manually inputting a web address or an input into a web interface is called "Scraping". This chapter will show you some techniques on how to do this and effectively merge this information into a spreadsheet that possibly has other data items, thus enriching the total information available in the document. The example used here is to demonstrate an automatic currency conversion. We use **Internet Explorer** for this example, as it is easily integrated into Excel. Other browsers can be used as well for this exercise, but they require a different code treatment not discussed here. I already hear some rumblings that this is not your preferred browser. The point is, once developed, this is pretty much invisible, so you do not have to physically interact with the browser at all. If you do use another browser, the code might look slightly different and may require other pieces of software to be installed. For example, using Google Chrome and Edge browsers require the installation of Selenium. Please see the resources page online for a code example using the Edge Browser.

9.1 ALGORITHM

The algorithm for the program works in three simple steps:

- Step 1—launch the web page
- Step 2—enter the currency pairs required from an input spreadsheet
- Step 3—get the exchange rate displayed and copy it into an output spreadsheet

DOI: 10.1201/9781003214335-10

We then repeat these steps until all currency codes from the input spreadsheet are exhausted.

In order to write the code, specific areas of the web page must be targeted. There are three areas that we are interested in:

- The field in which the currency code is entered (selection criteria field)
- The button which triggers the search (activation field)
- The field that stores the results (output field)

9.2   UNDERSTANDING THE HTML

This is critical because only through understanding the format can one read it correctly to be used in a program.

I used a technique described below.

Launch the webpage

Press F12 or go to tools—developer tools on your browser

Be sure to be on the Dom Explorer tab and enter Ctrl-B or click the circled button

As soon as you press it, the button is going to take you the original page. Use the crosshairs to click on the field you want to inspect. In this picture I clicked on the field that accepts input, see the red crosshairs that show up. As soon as I click, it takes me back to the developer view (see below)

This developer view now highlights the field you are interested in and shows us the details of how to identify it. For example, it shows that the **class** of this field is called "gLFyf gsfi"

HTML works in tags and it is hierarchical. Understanding this is key to writing a successful program.

Selection criteria field:

This can be easily identified by its Class ("gLFyf gsfi")

Trigger field:

This is the field called "Google Search" on the webpage. This is also identified by its Class. The first time you launch google this field belongs to class "gNO89b", but the second time onwards it is a different class field ("Tg7LZd")

9.3   OUTPUT FIELD

The output field is also identified a class value of "DFlfde SwHCTb". The value displayed by the webpage (the currency conversion rate) is accessed through a fieldname called "innertext".

In order to use the web processing HTML functions, the following options are necessary in the Excel VBA, accessed by the menu path Tools -> References in the VBA development screen.

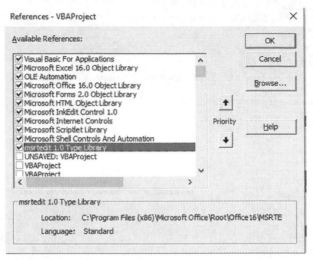

FIGURE 9.1 VBA References.

9.4   THE ALGORITHM

This is a simple program where we could identify the fields on the web page easily using just the class attribute. There are others that are more complex, and the field can be identified by alternative attributes. Some of these attributes are the id, the tag name, etc. These have not been covered here, but you are likely to need them when you deal with more complex web pages—google is probably one of the simplest by design, since it is a universal search application where most of its complexity resides on the server end.

The code for this algorithm is here:

```
Initialize variables and launch the website
Sub ScrapeWebsiteCurrency()
Dim ie As Object
Dim form As Variant
Dim button As Variant
Dim LR, RateRow As Integer
Dim var As String
Dim var1 As Object
Dim oHEle As HTMLULListElement ' Create HTML element (<ul>) object.
    LR = Worksheets("Currency Pairs").Cells(Rows.Count, 1).End(xlUp).Row
    RateRow = Worksheets("Currency Rates").Cells(Rows.Count, 1).End(xlUp).Row

    Set ie = CreateObject("internetexplorer.application")
    ie.Visible = True
    With ie
      .Visible = True
      .navigate "google.com/"
      While Not .readyState = READYSTATE_COMPLETE
```

STEP 1

STEP 1 continued	Wend End With 'Wait some to time for loading the page While ie.Busy DoEvents Wend Application.Wait (Now + TimeValue("0:00:02"))

STEP 2	***Get the input into the search field***
	For x = 2 To LR
	    var = Worksheets("Currency Pairs").Cells(x, 1).Value & ""&
	Worksheets("Currency Pairs").Cells(x, 2).Value
	
	    Set var1 = ie.document.getElementsByClassName("gLFyf gsfi")
	    AddressColumn = 2
	    ZipCodeColumn = 1
	    For Each one In var1
	    one.Value = var
	    Next one
	
	     'ie.document.getElementById("txtSearch").Value = var
	     'Here we are clicking on search Button
	    If x = 2 Then
	      Set cl_button = ie.document.getElementsByClassName("gNO89b")
	    For Each one In cl_button
	
	        one.Click
	        Exit For
	
	      Next one
	    Else
	      Set cl_button = ie.document.getElementsByClassName("Tg7LZd")
	      For Each one In cl_button
	
	        one.Click
	        Exit For
	      Next one
	      End If
	
	      While ie.Busy
	        DoEvents
	      Wend
	    :
	    :

Beginner's Guide to Code Algorithms

STEP 3	*Get the output into the spreadsheet. Note—the Wait command below to ensure the page has been given enough time to refresh before extracting the rate* ⋮ ⋮ ⋮ Application.Wait (Now + TimeValue("0:00:02")) Set cl_text = ie.document.getElementsByClassName("DFlfde SwHCTb") 　For Each one In cl_text 　　　　Worksheets("Currency Rates").Cells(RateRow + x - 1, 1).Value = Format(Date, "MM/DD/YYYY") 　　　　Worksheets("Currency Rates").Cells(RateRow + x - 1, 2).Value = Worksheets("Currency Pairs").Cells(x, 1).Value 　　　　Worksheets("Currency Rates").Cells(RateRow + x - 1, 3).Value = Worksheets("Currency Pairs").Cells(x, 2).Value 　　　　Worksheets("Currency Rates").Cells(RateRow + x - 1, 4).Value = one.innerText 　　　　　Exit For 　　Next one 　Next x 　ie.Quit 　Set ie = Nothing End Sub

9.5 CONCLUSION

This chapter is a vital stepping-stone to understanding the technique of automatically reading a web page and extracting the information into a spreadsheet.

You learned:

- How to read a web page
- How to identify tags
- How to use browser developer tools
- How to work with HTML
- How to use tags and extract information from inner texts

Connecting Excel with another application is a door to many possibilities, more of which is discussed in Chapter 10.

Here is an exercise for you—using the web scraping technique described in this chapter, prepare a list of your ten favorite cities and their maximum and minimum temperatures for today.

10 The Genius of Collaboration

Build a Burglar Alarm Using a Free Webcam Application

A famous cartoonist spent a lifetime developing a funny theme around collaborative machines. He developed 50,000 cartoons that explored the outrageous craft of Professor Butts—an eccentric scientist whose goal in life was to build a machine with unimaginable complexity for a simple task. His name is Rube Goldberg (1883–1970). His work continues through an extraordinary fan following of contemporary artists, writers, and cartoonists who celebrate his humor through their own creations!

FIGURE 10.1   Ultimate Coffee Machine.

DOI: 10.1201/9781003214335-11

Advance to 2020—the concept of collaborative machines is actually coming alive with the new technical capabilities of High Speed Internet, Artificial Intelligence, and Machine Learning. Take, for instance, the ability of a doctor to visit and diagnose a patient virtually—through the use of the video call capability of smartphones, where one smartphone (the doctor's) collaborates with the other (the patient's).

The pairing of technologies to deliver a difficult task has become the foundation of innovation in the business world today. Automakers are collaborating with cell phone companies to provide seamless voice call capability for drivers. Restaurants are working in partnership with transportation companies to carry their food to a customer who cannot travel. Banks are creating new products through joint ventures with airlines that allow passengers to spend money and earn points toward plane tickets.

In this spirit of collaborative tools, I wanted to introduce you to a few simple ideas that you can solve with your PC or laptop. My hope is that you find inspiration in these ideas to explore and innovate on your own to be the next Zuckerberg, or simply to enjoy the experience of doing something novel!

10.1   IDEAS

1. Burglar alarm
2. Counting the people who walk into your store or pass by your window
3. Taking a remote shot using googledocs
4. Greeting based on time of day

A fundamental component to make all these ideas work is a webcam software. There are many in the market. I particularly like Yawcam (www.yawcam.com) for its simplicity and the fact that it is free. The installation instructions are available from its website. Once installed, you have a control panel which you can configure. A quick discussion on these features below.

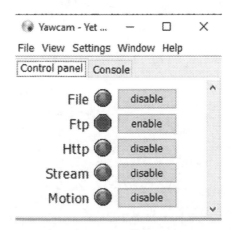

Motion—enables detection of motion by taking a snapshot.

This stores an image every time the camera detects motion in a folder of your choice.

Here are the settings for motion control.

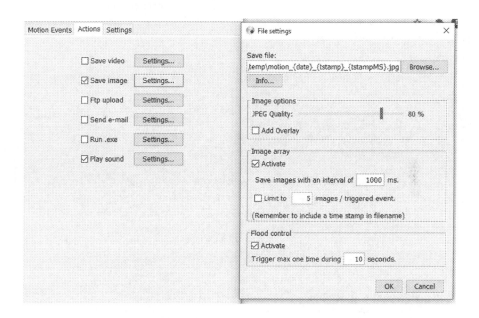

FIGURE 10.2 Settings of Yawcam.

10.2 BURGLAR ALARM

The settings are explained very well on their website. Note the naming convention for the images—this ensures that each image is date and time stamped so you can easily retrieve the ones you need. The flood control feature limits the snapshots so that you do not run out of disk space on your computer.

Also note the send email feature. Once motion has been detected, the software can automatically use your default email application and send a picture to your email id—which you can retrieve from your smartphone. This feature does not require any coding at all—perfect machine to machine collaboration that can serve you well as a burglar alarm if you set up in your home while you are away. This achieves our first goal.

10.3 COUNTING PEOPLE

To count the number of people who enter your store, you could use the same motion detection feature and count the number of files generated. The only problem is you might run out of space. To get over this problem it is possible to write a short program that maintains the number of pictures in a spreadsheet by date and then deletes the pictures. The code looks something like this (change the folder paths to your own):

```
PeopleInStore is the name of the worksheet.
Sub PeopleInStore()
   Dim FileItem As Object
   Dim SourceFolder As Object
   Folder = "C:\Users\deepa\Documents\webcam photo\Motion\temp" ' this is the
folder that has the motion detection pictures
   FolderNameIndex = 0
   PeopleCount = 0
   Set fs = CreateObject("Scripting.FileSystemObject")
   Set SourceFolder = fs.GetFolder(Folder)
   Worksheets("PeopleInStore").Cells(1,1).Value = "Date"
   Worksheets("PeopleInStore").Cells(NextAvailableRow, 1).Value = "Count"
   For Each FileItem In SourceFolder.Files
       PeopleCount = PeopleCount + 1
       FileItem.Delete
   Next
   NextAvailableRow = Worksheets("PeopleInStore").Cells(Rows.Count,
1).End(xlUp).Row
       Worksheets("PeopleInStore").Cells(NextAvailableRow, 1).Value = Format(Date,
"MM/DD/YYYY")
       Worksheets("PeopleInStore").Cells(NextAvailableRow, 2).Value = PeopleCount
End Sub
```

10.4 REMOTE PHOTO

The third objective was to take a remote photo shot using googledocs.

Here we use some assistance from the code we wrote in one of our previous chapters—Remote Control. Here we described how a googledocs document can be used to advance a slide in a powerpoint deck forward or backward. This is another example of collaborative design—we could use this same code but change the action from moving a slide to taking a picture.

The way to take a picture is to just start the Yawcam application. Because this has a feature to take a snap every so many seconds, configurable from the Settings menu.

All we need to do is start and stop the Yawcam application using googledocs, similar to how we advanced the slides in Chapter 4.

Here is the code to start the Yawcam application from a spreadsheet:

```
ShellExecute 0, "OPEN", "C:\Program Files (x86)\Yawcam\yawcam.exe", "",
"C:\Program Files (x86)\Yawcam\", 1
```

Here is the code to stop the Yawcam application:

```
Call Shell("TaskKill /Fi ""WindowTitle eq ""Yaw*"""""", 0)
```

10.5 TIME BASED GREETING

That brings us to our last objective—greeting based on time of day.

Imagine someone comes into your office or your apartment and as soon as the person walks in, the computer greets them with "Good Morning" or "Good Evening", etc. depending on the time of day.

You need two things here—identification that someone walked in—which is done by the first objective of motion detection. And then invoking the text-to-speech function. This simple code is provided below. It does need your laptop speaker so be sure to turn up your sound. We use a spreadsheet called "Greetings" with the following values:

File	Home	Insert	Page Layout	Formulas	Data	Review

A4   ▾   :   ✕   ✓   *fx*   Why are you still here - go home

	A	B	C	D	E
1	Good Morning				
2	Good Afternoon				
3	Good Evening				
4	Why are you still here - go home				
5					
6					

FIGURE 10.3   Text to speech.

STEP 1

Motion Detection.

```
Sub Greetings()

    Dim FileItem As Object
    Dim SourceFolder As Object
    x = Format(Time, "HH")
    Folder = "C:\Users\deepa\Documents\webcam photo\Motion\temp" ' this is the
folder that has the motion detection pictures
    Set fs = CreateObject("Scripting.FileSystemObject")
    Set SourceFolder = fs.GetFolder(Folder)
    MotionSensed = "N"
    For Each FileItem In SourceFolder.Files

    xdate = Format(Date, "MM/DD/YYYY")
    ydate = Format(FileDateTime(Folder & "\" & FileItem.Name), "MM/DD/YYYY")
    xhh = Format(Time, "HH")
    xmm = Format(Time, "MM")
    xtime = xhh * 60 + xmm
    Name = FileItem.Name
    yhh = Format(FileDateTime(Folder & "\" & FileItem.Name), "HH")
    ymm = Format(FileDateTime(Folder & "\" & FileItem.Name), "NN")
    ytime = yhh * 60 + ymm
    If xdate = ydate Then
        If xtime <= ytime + 1 Then
            MotionSensed = "Y"
        Else
        End If
    Else
        FileItem.Delete
    End If
Next
```

STEP 2	*Invoking text-to-speech function.*
	If MotionSensed = "Y" Then
	  If x < 12 Then
	    Worksheets("Greetings").Cells(1, 1).Speak
	  Else
	    If x < 16 Then
	      Worksheets("Greetings").Cells(2, 1).Speak
	    Else
	      If x < 18 Then
	        Worksheets("Greetings").Cells(3, 1).Speak
	      Else
	        Worksheets("Greetings").Cells(4, 1).Speak
	      End If
	    End If
	  End If
	End If
	End Sub

Once again—we see the powerful combination of the laptop and its speaker along with the camera producing a useful result for a user that puts collaboration to good use.

10.6   CONCLUSION

The three experiments shown in this chapter provide useful insight on what can be achieved through multiple systems interacting with each other. The possibilities are endless.

I invite you to consider other applications that can interact with Excel and build a collaboration scenario on your own.

11 Advanced Graphics

Complex Visualizations and More

A famous professor once said, "Calculus is the language of God" (Steven Strogatz—Infinite Possibilities). While I totally agree with that statement, discussing this is perhaps the topic for another day—perhaps you would like to read his book to understand why. But I think if calculus is the language of God, graphs are God's artwork. A graph can say so many things in a variety of ways! It gives us a new perspective that reveals impactful information that otherwise cannot be discovered easily from rows of numbers.

Take for instance this graph.

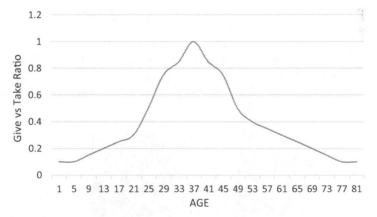

FIGURE 11.1   Magnanimity vs age.

It shows us how we depend on others in our early childhood and late maturity, but pretty much like to be in control for the period between youth and middle age.

Here are some more graphs representing life trends we are all too familiar with.

DOI: 10.1201/9781003214335-12

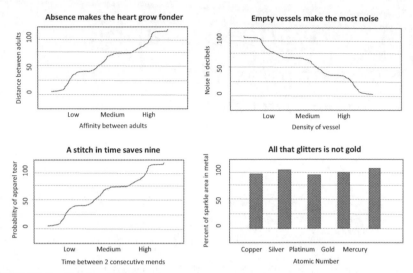

FIGURE 11.2   Graphs of life.

As I write this book, the world is suffering through a pandemic, the scale and impact of which has not happened to humanity in the past 100 years. The world leaders are trying to decide various aspects of their strategy to bring life back to normal. While there are many data items that are being measured and plotted, two key elements are the number of new infections and the number of deaths. This statistic is updated every day and is available in several public websites.

The data by itself are useless until we turn it into information that provides a perspective that becomes a basis for some serious decision-making action.

To convert data into information, you need a perspective. Think of perspective as a viewpoint—a certain angle from which you are looking at the situation. A couple of quick examples follow.

The four figures here represent the same pyramid but looked at from different angles.

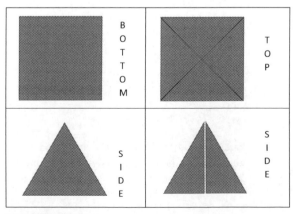

FIGURE 11.3   Views of a pyramid.

This picture looks like elephant grass and a giant white sheet for an ant.

ANT's EYE VIEW 1   ANT's EYE VIEW 2

FIGURE 11.4   Ant's eye view

Indeed, it is just a garden by the lakeside for a human being!

Human EYE VIEW 3   HUMAN EYE VIEW 4

FIGURE 11.5   Human eye view.

Many doctors and nurses lost their lives treating patients in the COVID-19 pandemic. I salute those fearless souls who put others' well-being ahead of their own! Preventing the spread of the virus is heavily dependent on reporting its impact. Many governments collected (and still collecting) these data from their medical communities and made them available for their citizens to raise awareness to encourage them to stay indoors.

This chapter shows you how to create a graph from the publicly available data that can provide you some perspective of the daily COVID infections and deaths in the United States. Here is why I chose this:

- It provides a good grounding on how to create charts
- It describes some easy techniques to get data from a website
- It helps you understand how to work with a map
- It provides insight into sorting techniques when you need numbers in a certain order

11.1   FEATURES OF THE GRAPH

Let's begin with the chart and then look at the other different features that are put together around it. Best done through an example, here is what we want.

A graph of number of COVID cases by US state (once you see the technique, you can easily extend it to other geographic regions around the world). We want it by day because that shows a clear trend (upward or downward). We want to see cumulative up to each date, as well as new cases separately because each means slightly different things in the trend chart. While most rely on this metric to determine how safe a place is, the other metric is number of deaths due to COVID. Deaths typically lag the infection by several weeks to several months, hence may not be the best indicator of safety, but certainly an indicator of other things such as the state's ability to handle cases, quality of care, and so on. It would be great to see comparisons of different states. Also, we would like to see the top N states so that that gives us a sense for the worst affected states.

We must remember that numbers are not everything—there are many factors involved in judging safety, and this analysis is just an experiment to help you develop charts. However, charts and graphs have a pretty loudmouth and tell a story that is worth a thousand words.

11.2   THE DATA

Before we begin, we have to get the data. Luckily, COVID data are publicly available from multiple sources and are updated on a daily basis. The source I have chosen for this exercise is https://usafactsstatic.blob.core.windows.net/public/data/covid-19. There are two files that are available in this web address:

- covid_confirmed_usafacts.csv
- covid_deaths_usafacts.csv

The names are self-explanatory.

Both these files have the same format as shown below, each cell showing the number of new cases in the days specified in the column header.

	A	B	C	D	E	F	G	H
1	countyFIPS	County Name	State	stateFIPS	1/22/2020	1/23/2020	1/24/2020	1/25/2020
2	0	Statewide Unallocated	AL	1	0	0	0	0
3	1001	Autauga County	AL	1	0	0	0	0
4	1003	Baldwin County	AL	1	0	0	0	0
5	1005	Barbour County	AL	1	0	0	0	0
6	1007	Bibb County	AL	1	0	0	0	0
7	1009	Blount County	AL	1	0	0	0	0
8	1011	Bullock County	AL	1	0	0	0	0
9	1013	Butler County	AL	1	0	0	0	0
10	1015	Calhoun County	AL	1	0	0	0	0
11	1017	Chambers County	AL	1	0	0	0	0
12	1019	Cherokee County	AL	1	0	0	0	0
13	1021	Chilton County	AL	1	0	0	0	0
14	1023	Choctaw County	AL	1	0	0	0	0
15	1025	Clarke County	AL	1	0	0	0	0
16	1027	Clay County	AL	1	0	0	0	0
17	1029	Cleburne County	AL	1	0	0	0	0

FIGURE 11.6   covid_confirmed_usafacts.csv.

11.3 THE USER INTERFACE

In order to drive the program with our choices, we come up with a design for the interface. Something simple like below. It has the choice of Cumulative vs Current (new) cases for selecting the top N. It also has the choice between cases and deaths. The Go button starts executing the code after the user has entered the input.

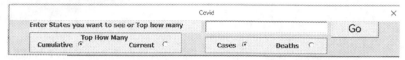

FIGURE 11.7   User interface for COVID graph.

We can enter the states with their two-character abbreviations with space separators like this:

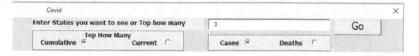

We can use the same input field to enter the top N—in the picture below N = 3:

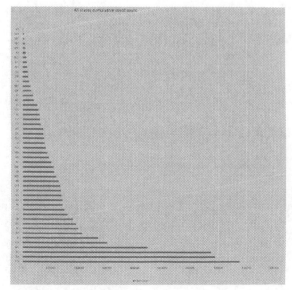

Here is the first chart we want.

11.4 THE BAR CHART

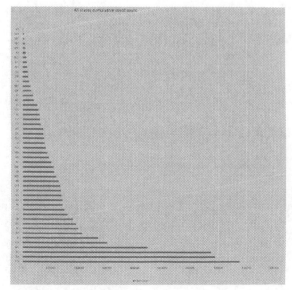

FIGURE 11.8   COVID infection by state.

This graph shows the cumulative count of COVID infections or deaths by state.

11.5   THE MAP CHART

The next graph we want is a graph of new infections or deaths to see the trend for multiple states.

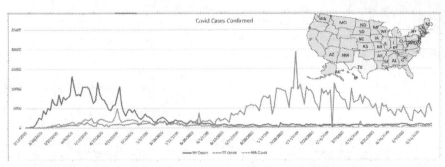

FIGURE 11.9   Graph of chosen states.

If we choose a top three instead of specific states, we would like to see a similar graph as above but want the code to figure out which out of 50 states are top three and show only those three states.

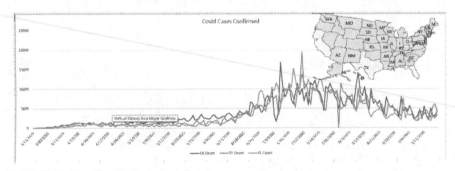

FIGURE 11.10   Graph of top three states.

11.6   THE ALGORITHM FOR THE CHART

Here is the algorithm for developing this chart.

Step 1
Set up the Form (user interface). To do this, you will need to follow the instructions that I described in Chapter 1. After you are done, you should have the following fields defined.

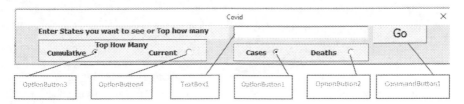

FIGURE 11.11   Form fields.

Step 2

Set up the sheets that you need to do the data manipulation. There are three sheets required:

- "Any State" which stores the data with dates in each row and states across the columns

	A	B	C	D	E	F	G
1		AL Count	AL Cum Count	AR Count	AR Cum Count	AZ Count	AZ Cum Count (
2	1/22/2020		0		0		0
3	1/23/2020	0	0	0	0	0	0
4	1/24/2020	0	0	0	0	0	0
5	1/25/2020	0	0	0	0	0	0
6	1/26/2020	0	0	0	0	1	1
7	1/27/2020	0	0	0	0	0	1

FIGURE 11.12   Any State.

- "States" that will store the state-level statistics

	A	B	C	D	E	F	G
1	State				State	Cum Cour	Rownum
2	AL				CA	775442	5
3	AR				TX	688128	44
4	AZ				FL	674456	10
5	CA				NY	447331	35
6	CO				GA	300903	11
7	CT				IL	268199	15
8	DC				AZ	211628	4
9	DE				NJ	198361	32
10	FL				NC	190742	28

FIGURE 11.13   State-level statistics.

- "Graphs" that will be used as the palette to show the charts we need as well as the US map.

Step 3
Invoke the form you created in step 1.

Step 4
Initialize variables and file paths, get the data from the website, load the US maps, and populate the data sheet in the format of the "Any State" sheet mentioned above.

Step 5
Sort the state-based summary in descending order.

Step 6
Draw the first chart (all states' cumulative COVID count).

Step 7
Draw the first state in the second chart.

Step 8
Add the other states to the second chart.

Here is the code:

```
Set up the sheets that you need to do the data manipulation.
Sub CovidGraphPrepare()
    Dim NewBook As Workbook
    Dim filepath As String
    Dim startrow(500) As Integer
    Dim rRange As Range
    Dim fileopenWb As Workbook, thisWb As Workbook
    Dim fileopenMapWb As Workbook
    Dim fileopenWs As Worksheet, thisWs As Worksheet
    StatesString = "AK,AL,AR,AZ,CA,CO,CT,DC,DE,FL,GA,HI,IA,ID,IL,IN,KS,KY,L
A,MA,MD,ME,MI,MN,MO, MS,MT,NC,ND,NE,NH,NJ,NM,NV,NY,OH,OK,OR,PA,R
I,SC,SD,TN,TX,UT,VA,VT,WA,WI,WV,WY"
    States = Split(StatesString, ",")
    ' Get a new Workbook
    If FirstTime = "Then
        Set NewBook = Workbooks.Add
        Do
            fName = Application.GetSaveAsFilename
        Loop Until fName <> False
        NewBook.SaveAs Filename:=fName
        CurrentWorkbookName = ActiveWorkbook.Name
        FirstTime = "N"
    End If

    ' Create all sheets required ***
    FoundSheet = 0
    For Each Sheet In ActiveWorkbook.Worksheets
```

STEP 2

<table>
<tr><td>

STEP 2 continued

</td><td>

```
        If Sheet.Name = "Any State" Then
            FoundSheet = 1
            Exit For
        End If
        Next
        If FoundSheet = 0 Then
            Set Sheet = ActiveWorkbook.Sheets.Add(After:=ActiveWorkbook.
Worksheets(ActiveWorkbook.Worksheets.Count))
            Sheet.Name = "Any State"
        End If
```

</td></tr>
<tr><td>

STEP 2 & 3

</td><td>

```
    FoundSheet = 0
    For Each Sheet In ActiveWorkbook.Worksheets
    If Sheet.Name = "States" Then
        FoundSheet = 1
        Exit For
    End If
    Next
    If FoundSheet = 0 Then
        Set Sheet = ActiveWorkbook.Sheets.Add(After:=ActiveWorkbook.
Worksheets(ActiveWorkbook.Worksheets.Count))
        Sheet.Name = "States"
    End If
    Worksheets("States").Cells(1, 1) = "State"
    Worksheets("States").Cells(1, 5) = "State"
    Worksheets("States").Cells(1, 6) = "Cum Count"
    Worksheets("States").Cells(1, 7) = "Rownum"
    For i = 1 To UBound(States)
        Worksheets("States").Cells(i + 1, 1) = States(i)
    Next


    FoundSheet = 0
    For Each Sheet In ActiveWorkbook.Worksheets
    If Sheet.Name = "Graphs" Then
        FoundSheet = 1
        Exit For
    End If
    Next
    If FoundSheet = 0 Then
        Set Sheet = ActiveWorkbook.Sheets.Add(After:=ActiveWorkbook.
Worksheets(ActiveWorkbook.Worksheets.Count))
        Sheet.Name = "Graphs"
    End If

    ' Sheets required End ***
    Workbooks(CurrentWorkbookName).Activate
    'MacroWorkBookName = ThisWorkbook.FullName

    UserForm1.Show
End Sub
```

</td></tr>
</table>

STEP 4

Initialize variables and file paths, get the data from the website, load the US, maps and populate the data sheet in the format of the "Any State" sheet mentioned above.

```vba
Public Declare PtrSafe Function GetKeyboardState Lib "user32" (pbKeyState As Byte) As Long
Public Declare PtrSafe Function GetAsyncKeyState Lib "User32.dll" (ByVal vKey As Long) As Long
Public States() As String
Public FirstTime As String
Public CurrentWorkbookName As String
Sub CovidGraph()
    Dim NewBook As Workbook
    Dim filepath As String
    Dim startrow(500) As Integer
    Dim rRange As Range
    Dim fileopenWb As Workbook, thisWb As Workbook
    Dim fileopenMapWb As Workbook
    Dim fileopenWs As Worksheet, thisWs As Worksheet
    Workbooks(CurrentWorkbookName).Activate
    'MacroWorkBookName = ThisWorkbook.FullName
    Set thisWb = ActiveWorkbook
    Set thisWs = thisWb.Sheets("Any State")
    Set thisWsGraphs = thisWb.Sheets("Graphs")
    If UserForm1.OptionButton1 = True Then
        ConfirmedOrDeaths = "C"
        thisWsGraphs.Cells(23, 3) = "Cases"
    Else
        ConfirmedOrDeaths = "D"
        thisWsGraphs.Cells(23, 3) = "Deaths"
    End If
        FileToValidate1 = "covid_confirmed_usafacts.csv"
        FileToValidate2 = "covid_deaths_usafacts.csv"

    If ConfirmedOrDeaths = "C" Then
        SheetToValidate = "covid_confirmed_usafacts"
        FileToValidate = "covid_confirmed_usafacts.csv"
    Else
        SheetToValidate = "covid_deaths_usafacts"
        FileToValidate = "covid_deaths_usafacts.csv"
    End If

    filepath = ActiveWorkbook.Path & "\" & FileToValidate
    filepath1 = ActiveWorkbook.Path & "\" & FileToValidate1
    filepath2 = ActiveWorkbook.Path & "\" & FileToValidate2
    filepathMap = ActiveWorkbook.Path & "\" & "USAMapCovid.xlsx"
```

STEP 4 continued (1)

```
Get the data from the website.
  Dim myURL As String
  Dim Days As Long

  Days = CLng(Format(Now, "YYYYMMDD")) - CLng(thisWsGraphs.Cells(23, 2))

   ' get the file of data from the web
  a = thisWsGraphs.Cells(23, 2)
  If CLng(Format(Now, "YYYYMMDD")) > 20200513 Then
     a = 1
  End If


  If Days > 0 Then
     myURL = "https://usafactsstatic.blob.core.windows.net/public/data/covid-19/
  covid_confirmed_usafacts.csv"
     Dim HttpReq As Object
     Set HttpReq = CreateObject("Microsoft.XMLHTTP")
      ' HttpReq.Open "GET", myURL, False, "username", "password"
     HttpReq.Open "GET", myURL, False, "", ""
     HttpReq.send
     myURL = HttpReq.responseBody
     If HttpReq.Status = 200 Then
     Set oStrm = CreateObject("ADODB.Stream")
     oStrm.Open
     oStrm.Type = 1
     oStrm.Write HttpReq.responseBody
     oStrm.SaveToFile filepath1, 2 ' 1 = no overwrite, 2 = overwrite
     oStrm.Close
     End If
  End If
  If Days > 0 Then
     myURL = "https://usafactsstatic.blob.core.windows.net/public/data/covid-19/
  covid_deaths_usafacts.csv"
     Set HttpReq = CreateObject("Microsoft.XMLHTTP")
      ' HttpReq.Open "GET", myURL, False, "username", "password"
     HttpReq.Open "GET", myURL, False, "", ""
     HttpReq.send
     myURL = HttpReq.responseBody
     If HttpReq.Status = 200 Then
       Set oStrm = CreateObject("ADODB.Stream")
       oStrm.Open
       oStrm.Type = 1
       oStrm.Write HttpReq.responseBody
       oStrm.SaveToFile filepath2, 2 ' 1 = no overwrite, 2 = overwrite
       oStrm.Close
     End If
  End If
```

STEP 4 continued (2)	**Load the US maps.**
	
	Do
	    On Error GoTo continue
	    Set fileopenMapWb = Workbooks.Open(filepathMap)
	    Exit Do
	continue:
	    filepathMapFuture = filepathMap
	    filepathMap = Application.GetOpenFilename
	    MsgBox ("Please identify the USAMapCovid.xlsx file you saved")
	    Set fileopenMapWb = Workbooks.Open(filepathMap)
	    fileopenMapWb.SaveAs Filename:=filepathMapFuture
	    Loop Until filepathMap <> False

11.7   BUILDING THE MAP

The US maps is a collection of 50 different shapes in MSDraw—each representing one state. The name of each shape is the same as the name of the state. These are all grouped together in a group called "Group 57" in the code (step 7) —you can change this name to your group as required in the code. This group needs to be in an Excel file called USAMapCovid.xlsx, in a sheet called "MAPS". The code above does provide for other names for this file, but this collection of 50 images is necessary to show the US map with the cool selection colors. Such groups are available through online vendors, or you can draw your own using standard drawing tools. (Hint: paste a picture of the US map and draw over it using MSDraw Freeform Shape tool that looks like a scribble:

STEP 4 continued (3)	**Populate the data sheet in the format of the "Any State" sheet mentioned above.**
	
	Set fileopenWb = Workbooks.Open(filepath)
	 'Workbooks(FileToValidate).Activate
	Set fileopenWs = fileopenWb.Sheets(SheetToValidate)
	 'thisWb is the analysis workbook
	thisWs.Range("A2:A1000", "B1:JZ1000").ClearContents
	thisWsGraphs.Activate
	For Each Shp In ActiveSheet.Shapes
	   Shp.Delete
	Next Shp
	NumberOfRows = fileopenWs.Cells(Rows.Count, 1).End(xlUp).Row
	NumberOfCols = fileopenWs.Cells(1, Columns.Count).End(xlToLeft).Column
	 'thisWs.Cells(1, 1) = 1
	 'fileopenWs.Cells(1, 1) = 1
	
	NumberOfStates = thisWb.Sheets("States").Cells(Rows.Count, 1).End(xlUp).
	Row - 1 'compensating for header row
	   fileopenWs.Activate
	   j = 1
	   k = 0

| **STEP 4 continued (3)** | ```
For i = 1 To 100
   startrow(i) = 2
Next

For i = 5 To NumberOfCols
   j = j + 1
   thisWs.Cells(j, 1) = Format(fileopenWs.Cells(1, i), "MM/DD/YYYY")
   For kk = 1 To NumberOfStates
   k = 1 + 2 * (kk - 1)
   thisWs.Cells(j, k + 2) = Application.SumIf(Range(Cells(2, 3),
Cells(NumberOfRows, 3)), thisWb.Sheets("States").Cells(kk + 1, 1), Range(Cells(2, i),
Cells(NumberOfRows, i)))
   If j > 2 Then
      thisWs.Cells(j, k + 1) = thisWs.Cells(j, k + 2) - thisWs.Cells(j - 1, k + 2)
   If startrow(kk) = 2 And thisWs.Cells(j, k + 2) > 0 Then
      startrow(kk) = j
   End If
Else
      thisWs.Cells(1, k + 1) = thisWb.Sheets("States").Cells(kk + 1, 1) & " Count"
      thisWs.Cells(1, k + 2) = thisWb.Sheets("States").Cells(kk + 1, 1) & "
Cum Count"
   End If
   Next
Next
``` |
| **STEP 5** | ***Sort state-based summaries in descending order.***

```
'find top 10
   If UserForm1.OptionButton3 = True Then
      For i = 1 To NumberOfStates
         thisWb.Sheets("States").Cells(i + 1, 5) = thisWb.Sheets("States").Cells(i + 1, 1)
         thisWb.Sheets("States").Cells(i + 1, 6) = thisWb.Sheets("Any State").Cells(j, 3
+ 2 * (i - 1))
         thisWb.Sheets("States").Cells(i + 1, 7) = i + 1
      Next
   Else
         thisWb.Sheets("States").Cells(1, 6) = "Curr count"
For i = 1 To NumberOfStates
         thisWb.Sheets("States").Cells(i + 1, 5) = thisWb.Sheets("States").Cells
(i + 1, 1)
         thisWb.Sheets("States").Cells(i + 1, 6) = thisWb.Sheets("Any State").Cells(j, 2
+ 2 * (i - 1))
         thisWb.Sheets("States").Cells(i + 1, 7) = i + 1
      Next
   End If

   thisWb.Worksheets("States").Sort.SortFields.Add2 Key:=Range("F2:F52") _
   , SortOn:=xlSortOnValues, Order:=xlDescending, DataOption:=xlSortNormal
``` |
```

STEP 5 continued	With thisWb.Worksheets("States").Sort
	    .SetRange Range("E1:G52")
	    .Header = xlYes
	    .MatchCase = False
	    .Orientation = xlTopToBottom
	    .SortMethod = xlPinYin
	    .Apply
	End With

STEP 6	***Draw the first chart (all states' cumulative COVID count).***
	    ' First overall graph
	    thisWsGraphs.Activate
	
	    NameOfOverallChart = "All states cumulative covid count"
	    ActiveSheet.Shapes.AddChart2(216, xlBarClustered).Select
	    ActiveChart.SetSourceData Source:=Range("States!$E$1:$F$52")
	    ActiveChart.ChartType = xlBarClustered
	     'ActiveChart.ChartType = xlColumnClustered
	    ActiveChart.Parent.Name = NameOfOverallChart
	    ActiveChart.ChartTitle.Text = NameOfOverallChart
	    ActiveSheet.Shapes(NameOfOverallChart).Left = 50
	    ActiveSheet.Shapes(NameOfOverallChart).Top = 1
	    ActiveSheet.Shapes(NameOfOverallChart).ScaleWidth 0.5, msoFalse,
	msoScaleFromTopLeft
	    ActiveSheet.Shapes(NameOfOverallChart).ScaleHeight 1, msoFalse,
	msoScaleFromBottomRight
	    ActiveSheet.ChartObjects(NameOfOverallChart).Chart.HasLegend = True
	    ActiveSheet.ChartObjects(NameOfOverallChart).Chart.Legend.
	Position = xlBottom
	    ActiveSheet.Shapes(NameOfOverallChart).Fill.ForeColor.
	ObjectThemeColor = msoThemeColorAccent4
	    ActiveChart.Axes(xlValue).MajorGridlines.Select

STEP 7	***Draw the first state in the second chart.***
	    TopHowMany = UserForm1.TextBox1.Value
	    If TopHowMany = "" Then
	       TopHowMany = 5
	    End If
	    Dim SpecificState() As String
	    SpecificState = Split(TopHowMany)
	    SpecificStateColumn = ""
	    For m = 1 To NumberOfStates
	      a = InStr(1, SpecificState(0), thisWb.Sheets("States").Cells(1 + m, 1), 1)
	      If a > 0 Then
	         SpecificState(0) = Mid(SpecificState(0), 1, 2)
	         SpecificStateColumn = m
	      End If
	    Next
	    ErrorInput = "N"
	    If SpecificStateColumn = "" And (TopHowMany < 0 Or TopHowMany > 52) Then

STEP 7 continued

```
            UserForm1.TextBox1.ForeColor = vbRed
            UserForm1.Caption = " COVID - Wrong input: Try Again!"
            ErrorInput = "Y"
        End If
        If ConfirmedOrDeaths = "C" Then
            NameOfChart = "Covid Cases Confirmed"
        Else
            NameOfChart = "Covid Deaths Confirmed"
        End If
        ActiveSheet.Shapes.AddChart2(227, xlLine).Select
        If SpecificState(0) = "" Or SpecificStateColumn = "" Then
            mm = thisWb.Sheets("States").Cells(2, 7) - 1
        Else
            mm = SpecificStateColumn
        End If
        ActiveChart.SetSourceData Source:=Range(thisWs.Cells(startrow(1), 2 * mm),
thisWs.Cells(j, 2 * mm))
        ActiveChart.Parent.Name = NameOfChart
        ActiveChart.ChartTitle.Text = NameOfChart
        ActiveSheet.Shapes(NameOfChart).Left = 1
        ActiveSheet.Shapes(NameOfChart).Top = 1
        ActiveSheet.Shapes(NameOfChart).ScaleWidth 2.7, msoFalse, _
            msoScaleFromTopLeft
        ActiveSheet.Shapes(NameOfChart).ScaleHeight 1.5, msoFalse, _
            msoScaleFromBottomRight
        ActiveSheet.ChartObjects(NameOfChart).Chart.HasLegend = True
        ActiveSheet.ChartObjects(NameOfChart).Chart.Legend.Position = xlBottom
        ActiveChart.Axes(xlValue).MajorGridlines.Select
```

Continue drawing the first state in the second chart.
```
        Set rRange = Range(thisWs.Cells(1, 2 * mm), thisWs.Cells(1, 2 * mm))
        ActiveChart.SeriesCollection(1).Name = "='Any State'!" & rRange.Address(True,
True, xlR1C1)
        Set rRange = Range(thisWs.Cells(startrow(1), 2 * mm), thisWs.Cells(j, 2 * mm))
        ActiveChart.SeriesCollection(1).Values = "='Any State'!" & rRange.Address(True,
True, xlR1C1)
        Set rRange = Range(thisWs.Cells(startrow(1), 1), thisWs.Cells(j, 1))
        ActiveChart.SeriesCollection(1).XValues = "='Any State'!" & rRange.
Address(True, True, xlR1C1)
```

Paint the US map.
```
        ' First get the map
        fileopenMapWb.Sheets("MAPS").Shapes("Group 57").Copy
        fileopenMapWb.Close
        thisWsGraphs.Activate
        thisWsGraphs.Range("o1").Select
        ActiveSheet.Paste
```

STEP 7 continued	thisWsGraphs.Shapes(thisWsGraphs.Shapes.Count).Select Selection.ShapeRange.ScaleWidth 0.35, msoFalse, msoScaleFromTopLeft Selection.ShapeRange.ScaleHeight 0.3, msoFalse, msoScaleFromTopLeft Selection.ShapeRange.ZOrder msoBringToFront StateExists = ShapeColor(Left(thisWs.Cells(1, 2 * mm), 2)) thisWsGraphs.Shapes(NameOfChart).Select ActiveChart.FullSeriesCollection(1).Select

STEP 8	***Add the other states to the second chart. Note the use of the variable SpecificStateColumn to determine if this is a "Top x" graph or a graph of specific states requested by the user.***
	
	If ErrorInput = "N" Then
	If SpecificStateColumn = "" Then
	  jj = 1
	    For m = 2 To TopHowMany
	      mm = thisWb.Sheets("States").Cells(1 + m, 7) - 1
	      jj = jj + 1
	      thisWsGraphs.Shapes(NameOfChart).Select
	      ActiveChart.SeriesCollection.Add Source:=Range(thisWs.Cells(startrow(1), 2 * mm), thisWs.Cells(j, 2 * mm))
	      Set rRange = Range(thisWs.Cells(1, 2 * mm), thisWs.Cells(1, 2 * mm))
	      ActiveChart.SeriesCollection(jj).Name = "='Any State'!" & rRange.Address(True, True, xlR1C1)
	      Set rRange = Range(thisWs.Cells(startrow(1), 1), thisWs.Cells(j, 1))
	      ActiveChart.SeriesCollection(jj).XValues = "='Any State'!" & rRange.Address(True, True, xlR1C1)
	      StateExists = ShapeColor(Left(thisWs.Cells(1, 2 * mm), 2))
	    Next
	  Else
	    jj = 1
	    For m = 1 To UBound(SpecificState)
	      If SpecificState(m) = "" Then
	        Exit For
	      End If
	        SpecificStateColumn = ""
	        For n = 1 To NumberOfStates
	      a = InStr(1, SpecificState(m), thisWb.Sheets("States").Cells(1 + n, 1), 1)
	        If a > 0 Then
	          SpecificState(m) = Mid(SpecificState(m), 1, 2)
	          SpecificStateColumn = n
	        End If
	      Next
	      If SpecificStateColumn <> "" Then
	        mm = SpecificStateColumn
	        jj = jj + 1
	        thisWsGraphs.Shapes(NameOfChart).Select
	        ActiveChart.SeriesCollection.Add Source:=Range(thisWs.Cells(startrow(1), 2 * mm), thisWs.Cells(j, 2 * mm))

STEP 8 continued	Set rRange = Range(thisWs.Cells(1, 2 * mm), thisWs.Cells(1, 2 * mm)) ActiveChart.SeriesCollection(jj).Name = "='Any State'!" & rRange. Address(True, True, xlR1C1) Set rRange = Range(thisWs.Cells(startrow(1), 1), thisWs.Cells(j, 1)) ActiveChart.SeriesCollection(jj).XValues = "='Any State'!" & rRange. Address(True, True, xlR1C1) StateExists = ShapeColor(Left(thisWs.Cells(1, 2 * mm), 2)) End If Next End If End If ActiveSheet.Shapes(NameOfOverallChart).ZOrder msoBringToFront ActiveSheet.Cells(23, 2) = Format(Now, "YYYYMMDD") fileopenWb.Close (True) End Sub

Other Functions	*These are functions that are called from the code and from the form elements.*
	Function ShapeColor(Label)
	Dim ashp As Shape
	On Error GoTo error_handler:
	ShapeExists = True
	ActiveSheet.Shapes(Label).Select
	Selection.ShapeRange(1).Fill.ForeColor.RGB = RGB(255, 255, 0)
	Exit Function
	error_handler:
	ShapeExists = False
	End Function
	Private Sub OptionButton1_Click()
	UserForm1.OptionButton2 = False
	End Sub
	Private Sub OptionButton2_Click()
	UserForm1.OptionButton1 = False
	End Sub
	Private Sub OptionButton3_Click()
	UserForm1.OptionButton4 = False
	End Sub
	Private Sub OptionButton4_Click()
	UserForm1.OptionButton3 = False
	End Sub
	Private Sub TextBox1_Change()
	UserForm1.TextBox1.ForeColor = vbBlack
	UserForm1.Caption = " Covid"
	a = InStr(1, UserForm1.TextBox1, "*")
	If a = 0 Then
	a = InStr(1, UserForm1.TextBox1, ".")
	End If

<table>
<tr><td rowspan="1">Other Functions continued</td><td>

```
    If a > 0 Then
        UserForm1.TextBox1 = Left(UserForm1.TextBox1, Len(UserForm1.
TextBox1) - 1)
        Call CovidGraph
    End If
End Sub
Private Sub TextBox1_KeyDown(ByVal KeyCode As MSForms.ReturnInteger, ByVal
Shift As Integer)
        If KeyCode = 13 Then
            Call CovidGraph
        End If
End Sub
```

</td></tr>
</table>

11.8   CONCLUSION

Drawing graphical representations of data is a powerful way to communicate. This chapter provides you with some advanced techniques on how to develop a visualization of data that is available freely.

You learned several advanced techniques to:

- Plot graphs
- Build forms
- Retrieve and categorize high volumes of data
- Plot the data on a map

I invite you to extend this code to include the county information that is also available from the website provided here.

The Final Word

This book is meant to motivate and inspire. While each chapter describes a different problem, there is an underlying theme that you would have observed—that "common sense" can be augmented to do superior things. Being able to write a program gives you the ability to transform a mind-boggling problem to a series of steps that will ultimately lead you to the solution. Writing a program is a one-time effort which can save you many hours of mundane and repetitive work.

I hope you will be inspired to look at a mundane task in your daily routine and pause to ask yourself "Why am I doing this again? Is there a better way to do this? Can I ask my computer to do it?"

If you are a person who loves solving riddles, this is a perfect book for you to be entertained by the numerous puzzles discussed in this book. The problems discussed are universal. The solutions are based on a coding platform that is already available to you if you are a Microsoft Excel user. The code solutions provided work best on Windows systems and have been tested in Windows 10. That being said, they should work in earlier versions with minor edits.

I have described the algorithms to a point where you will enjoy solving the enigma yourself. At the end of each chapter, there are a few problems to kindle your curiosity and extend your augmented common sense (ACS). These exercises will unlock your problem-solving skills and help you discover the power of logic.

If you are a smart new age reader, you may be on this page already, trying to find out why you should be reading this book. My advice to you is that you read each chapter in sequence since the chapters are arranged in an increasing order of difficulty. And also, the fun of learning programming is in doing it rather than reading it. All the codes in this book are original—written by me—and available for you to download and modify as needed. Try the code on your computer as you continue to progress through your chapters. Most readers will want to read the chapters a few times to test out the ideas discussed. Some readers will probably want to further develop the ideas presented here, and some of those improvements may lead to great innovations of the future!

Figures

Bibliography

1. Getting Started with VBA in Office https://docs.microsoft.com/en-us/office/vba/library-reference/concepts/getting-started-with-vba-in-office
2. Office VBA reference https://docs.microsoft.com/en-us/office/vba/api/overview/
3. Excel VBA Reference https://docs.microsoft.com/en-us/office/vba/api/overview/excel
4. Stephen Strogatz, "Infinite Possibilities"
5. Yawcam – Yet Another Webcam Software www.yawcam.com/

A Little Bit of Computer Science

Listed below are the simple concepts that have been used in the programs described in this book.

This list is not meant to be a complete list of features available in Excel VBA

Activate	A statement to make an object active. For example, Workbooks(CurrentWorkbookName).Activate makes the worksheet that is stored in CurrentWorbookName variable Active.
ActiveChart	The chart that is currently active
ActivePresentation	The presentation object in powerpoint that is currently active (being shown on the screen)
Add Operation	Add two operands
AddCallout	A statement used in VBA to add a callout box to a presentation
Application.Statusbar	The area at the bottom of a screen
Array	A set of variables that can be called by an index. This provides the unique opportunity to maintain a sequence in which a collection of variables is stored or used. For example, instead of using A, B, C, D,… as variable names you could use ALPHA(1), ALPHA(2), ALPHA(3), ALPHA(4)…
BeginArrowheadStyle	The style of the arrow head of a line at its top
BODMAS	A rule that is followed to control the order of calculation in an expression B = Bracket (parentheses) O = Of (Exponent)
Button	User interface item available on the form
Call statement	A statement that calls a set of other statements that are organized to do a specific set of tasks. Parameters can be passed to these tasks through variables. When parameters are passed there are two ways that the statements in the "Call" block use them By value, meaning it adopts the value passed during the call and does not retain the value after the call is complete By reference, which means it adopts the last assigned value to this variable and retains the value if it is changed in the "Call" block after the call is complete

Cells	A reference to a cell on the spreadsheet. CELLS(x,y) is the value in row x and column y
Chart	graph
Click	Used to simulate a click on a website
Close	A statement that closes the file
CommandButton	A form button that can execute a macro by clicking it
Comment	A description in the code to enhance its documentation. It is written with a preceding apostrophe ('). All test after an apostrophe in the same line becomes a comment. If the first non-blank character in a line is an apostrophe, then the whole line is a comment.
Conditional Statement	See IF Statement
Const	A statement to declare a constant
CreateObject	A statement to create an instance of an object
Data type	The type of data of a variable. The basic data types are: Integer—no decimals (4 bytes) Long—larger integer (8 bytes) Single—decimal (4bytes) Double—decimal (8 bytes) String—characters (up to 65400) Boolean—True or False
Declaration	A concept of declaring the type and dimension of the variables that will be used in a program. Visual Basic does not need variables to be declared unless they are arrays. But it is a good practice to declare all variables. If a variable is not declared, its type is assumed by the operation. For example,
Delete	Remove object
Dim Statement	A statement that declares the type of a variable
Dimension of Array	Number of memory units assigned to an array. An array is a set of variables that can be read and manipulated together. The dimension is the maximum number of units in this set. The first member of this set is A(0) where A is the array If the dimension is N then the last member of this set is A(N-1)
Dir Function	A function that identifies the folder structure beneath a given starting point. It behaves very similarly to the DIR in MSDOS or the Windows Command Prompt
Divide Operation	Divide two operands and store the value in the target variable format The value is truncated if the target variable is of type integer For example, X = Y/2 If X is defined as an integer and Y is 11 then X will assume a value of 5 after this operation.
Else Statement	A part of an IF statement that executes if the IF condition fails

End Function	Signifies the end point of a function that is called by a program
End If	Signifies the end point of an if statement in a program
EndArrowheadStyle	The style of the arrow head of a line at its bottom
Exit	A statement that tells the processor to come out of a loop (IF, WEND, etc…)
Exit Sub	A statement that tells the processor to stop executing the program that is currently being executed—control passes to the calling program or if this is the first program then the program stops
Exponentiation operation	Raises a variable to the power of another For example, $2^3 = 2 \times 2 \times 2 = 3$
Flag	Use of a variable with only 2 values to designate "ON" or "OFF" Very effective in checking binary conditions that have Yes/No answers such as: Did I find my word in this list? Was there an error in the calculation?
For Statement	A type of statement that allows for a controlled repetition of a group of statements. The control is in the very first statement as in the example below, variable I is tested to check if it is between 1 and 100 For I = 1 to 100 \<statement> \<statement> : \<statement> Next
ForeColor	Foreground color
Form	A collection of fields organized in an aesthetically pleasant way to help a person enter information for further processing by the program
Format function	Convert text in a specific way
FullScreen	A function that makes a window display in full screen
Function	A subroutine that passes back a value as part of its name. It is similar to a subroutine, but can be used in a calling program to decipher a value passed by the called program as part of its name.
googledocs	The visual text editing tool that Google provides
GoTo	A statement that passes control to another part of the code. Typically used as an error handling mechanism—if used in conjunction with On Error statement the control passes to this line if the processor encounters an error condition (such as division by zero)
HTML	Hypertext Markup Language— used to read a website
HttpReq	Request to retrieve a web page

If Statement	A conditional statement that is executed only if a condition is fulfilled. Its syntax is
	If <condition > then
	<statement>
	Else
	<statement>
	End If

Index	Also a variable, must be numeric Its sole purpose is to provide the sequence for an array For example, ALPHA(I) is an array and I is its index. It can be varied from 0 to N, N being the number of cells it is designed to have. The limit N is set by the Dim statement
Initialization	Setting of values at the beginning of a program. Generally speaking, a variable, whether declared or undeclared in VBA, assumes a value of null if string and zero if numeric.
Instr function	A statement to find at what position a sub-string occurs in a string. For example, INSTR ("ABCDE","CDE") returns the number 3 because CDE is in the third position in the string "ABCDE". If the string is not found, the value returned is zero.
Iteration counter	A variable used to keep track of how many times a set of statements has been executed. For I = 1 to 100 <statement> <statement> : <statement> Next I is the iteration counter in the example above and is automatically incremented by 1
Iterative statement	See FOR statement
Label	Attribute f a graphical element
Modulus Operation	Divides 2 operands and identifies the remainder
MsgBox	A message that is displayed on the screen. It has only one parameter—a string variable.
Multiply Operation	Multiply two operands
Next statement	The ending statement of a For Loop Once the system encounters this statement, it completes one iteration and goes in for the next after checking the iteration condition.
Object	A generic name for items with complex structures that cannot be described with a simple data type. For example, a workbook is an object and the worksheet is also an object
On Error	A statement to detect any error that takes place in the next statement without knowing what error it is. Used with RESUME or GOTO.

Open	A statement that opens a file with a given directory path name
Operation	An operation is a programming construct that denotes a simple action with variables and/or constants

An operation can be

Add
Subtract
Multiply
Divide
Modulus
Exponentiation
Example:
variable X=5 and variable Y=10

Operator	Description	Example
+	Adds the two operands	X+Y = 15
-	Subtracts the second operand from the first	X-Y = 5
*	Multiplies both the operands	X*Y = 50
/	Divides the numerator by the denominator	X/Y = 2
%	Modulus operator and the remainder after an integer division	X%Y = 0
^	Exponentiation operator	Y^X = 100000

OptionButton	Button on a form that is part of a set that functions like radio buttons—i.e. only one in the set can be selected
Parameter	Values that are passed to a block of code that is referred to as a Subroutine (Sub) or Function
Public	A variable declaration that is valid across all subroutines and functions. Normally, a variable is only available in a program and not in the program it calls. A variable declared with PUBLIC is available everywhere until execution stops
Recursion	Code that calls itself repetitively in a controlled manner
Select	Used along with the name of an object such as a sheet or a range, this verb has the same effect as selecting multiple cells in a spreadsheet. You can take action on this set of cells by referring to the selected objects as a "selection"
Selection	The selected set of objects after executing a "select" statement
Set	A statement to assign a constant to a variable
Sheets	Worksheet reference
ShellExecute	Execute an operating system command outside excel
Show	Display
ShowType	The type of presentation of a powerpoint deck
Sleep	A function that is used to pause processing for N seconds where N is a number defined in the sleep statement—sleep(N)

SlideShowWindow	The window in which the powerpoint presentation is being presented
Sub	A subroutine that holds the code that a macro executes
Subtract Operation	Subtract two operands
Tags	Used to identify a section of the web page
TextBox	A box that contains text. The text in the box can be set through a variable in a program A graphical object that is rectangular
TextFrame2	Attribute that allows you to read the text in a graphical shape
Variable	A temporary storage location for a data value. Represented by a string of alphanumeric characters Cannot have a space in between Used for moving values from one place to another
Visible	A function that makes an object visible
Weight	The thickness of a line
Wend	The end of a While statement
While	An iteration technique that checks a value rather than a counter Example: While I < 100 <statement> <statement> : <statement> Wend The difference from the FOR statement is that there are no automatic counters. In the example above, one has to increment the variable I in one of the statements in the loop.
Workbook	A collection of worksheets
Workbooks.Open	Open a workbook to read or write its content
Worksheet	The sheet or sheets that make up the workbook
Write	A statement to write a line on the file. Each write statement writes one record.
Yawcam	Yet another webcam—free webcam software

Index

Printed in the United States
by Baker & Taylor Publisher Services